EXECUTIVE SUCCESS

ADMINISTRATION SERIES

Eugene E. Jennings, *Editor*

Basic Computer Programming	*Decima M. Anderson*
Cases in Personnel Management and Supervision	*Richard P. Calhoon*
Personnel Management and Supervision	*Richard P. Calhoon*
Business Policies and Decision Making	*Raymond J. Ziegler*
Management in International Perspective	*S. Benjamin Prasad*
Measuring Executive Effectiveness	*Frederic R. Wickert & Dalton E. McFarland*
Executive Success	*Eugene E. Jennings*

EUGENE EMERSON JENNINGS
MICHIGAN STATE UNIVERSITY

Executive Success:
Stresses, Problems, and Adjustment

NEW YORK

APPLETON-CENTURY-CROFTS
Division of Meredith Publishing Company

Copyright © 1967 by
MEREDITH PUBLISHING COMPANY
All rights reserved

This book, or parts thereof, must not be used or reproduced in any manner without written permission. For information address the publisher, Appleton-Century-Crofts, Division of Meredith Publishing Company, 440 Park Avenue South, New York, N.Y. 10016

687–1

Library of Congress Card Number: 67–27560

ACKNOWLEDGMENTS

The cases of Mark Whiting, Sam, Norman, Neal, Stan, George, Paul, Bill, Henry, and John and the illustrations of the "Corporate Triangle," including "AC," "OC," "SC," and the "AOS Triad" are from Eugene Emerson Jennings' *The Executive in Crisis*, published by the Bureau of Business and Economic Research, Michigan State University. Copyright © 1965 by the Board of Trustees of Michigan State University.

PRINTED IN THE UNITED STATES OF AMERICA

E48070

To Ruth and Ted

PREFACE

This book is a revision and enlargement of a book entitled *The Executive in Crisis* published by the Bureau of Business and Economic Research, Graduate School of Business Administration, Michigan State University. In this present book the theoretical language and the references to scholarly studies have been deleted entirely.

However, the author wishes to acknowledge his special indebtedness to the works of W. L. Warner, *Big Business Leaders of America*, Harper, 1960, and Karen Horney, *Neurosis and Human Growth*, Norton, 1964. Professor Warner has provided research material about the mobility and achievement drives of big business executives. The author has adopted the neurotic defense mechanisms of aggression, effacement and resignation from the psychoanalytical formulations of Dr. Horney.

The earlier book was based upon fifteen cases of presidents and vice presidents who came to the author for professional counseling. After their therapy was completed, their cases were thoroughly documented by an investigation of the leading characters of their career crises. The relevant facts were incorporated into a composite profile and when there were differences of opinion among the central figures in the executive's crisis situation, the author served as the arbitrator. The present volume has incorporated four new composite profiles of executives in crisis, and the former cases have been enlarged and more systematically analyzed to give the reader a more practical understanding of executives who have succeeded in one sense and failed in another sense.

The composite profiles are represented by a single asterisk (*). The cases marked by a double asterisk (**) represent digested case histories that have been documented or are being documented. These brief histories are presented to illustrate special problems that arise in counseling crisis stricken executives and are found in Chapter 4, "What to do until the counselor comes." In both the composite profiles and brief case histories, the names of the executives and identifiable aspects of their corporate circumstances have been changed to preserve anonymity.

The author is indebted to Leo G. Erikson, Director of the Bureau of Business and Economic Research, for giving his support for this revision and enlargement. He is indebted to Orvis and June Collins, both of whom are Professors of Sociology at Southern Illinois University and who, as friends and colleagues, gave vital recommendations to the author about presenting the case data.

The author is indebted to his wife, Marilynne, for her professional assistance in helping to gather and compile case data and for typing and editing the manuscript.

E. E. J.

CONTENTS

Preface		vii
1	WHEN THE TOP RUNG BREAKS ON THE CORPORATE LADDER	1
	The Case of Mark Whiting	2
2	THE MAKING OF AN EXECUTIVE	18
	Arriving Is Departing	20
	The Pull of the Executive Group	22
	Why Executives Keep an Eye on Themselves	25
	The Need for Autonomy and Integrity	28
	What Whiting Lacked	31
3	I WOULD RATHER BE DEAD THAN A FAILURE	34
	The Case of Will Fowler	37
	The Recovery of Will Fowler	47
4	WHAT TO DO UNTIL THE COUNSELOR COMES	52

	The Causes of a Career Crisis	55
	Shame and Guilt Anxiety	58
	Executive Isolation	63
	Cue Anxiety	67
	Career Defense	70
	Lost Reality	73
5	WHY EXECUTIVES REBEL OR CONFORM	78
	How the Corporate Triangle Aids Mobility	79
	The Case of Hawley Simpson	84
	The Case of Alvin Peck	89
	Peck, Simpson, and Fowler Compared	91
6	THE UNBELIEVER AND THE CORPORATE CONSCIENCE	93
	The Organizing Drive	93
	The Case of Oscar Hanson	97
	The Case of Olaf Johnson	101
7	THE PERILS OF THE SELFISH SELF	109
	The Power of the Self-Image	110
	The Case of Sam Cory	115
	The Case of Oliver Dansby	121
	Why the Wrong Men Get to the Top	132
8	THE CRISIS OF THE LAST STEP	138
	The Committed Executive	140
	The Case of Jonathan Barr	142

	The "Success in Any Role" Type	148
	The Committed and Associated Types Compared	153
	How the Committed and Associated Handle Anxiety	155
9	**THE NEUROCRATIC EXECUTIVE**	**160**
	The Inside and Outside Solutions	161
	The Defenses of a Neurotic Executive	163
	Norman the Neurocrat	170
	Neal the Neurocrat	174
	Mr. Inside and Mr. Outside Compared	177
10	**THE FAILURE PRONE EXECUTIVE**	**181**
	How Executives Become Victimized	181
	Mark Whiting's Style of Panic	188
	The Victim's Fear of Failure	191
	The Victim's Illusion of Immunity	193
	The Victim's Illusion of Mastery	194
	The Victim's Illusion of Support	196
	The Victim's Illusion of Explanation	197
	The Victim's Unbalanced Triangle	198
	Conclusion: The Tyranny of the Success Habit	200

1

WHEN THE TOP RUNG BREAKS
ON THE CORPORATE LADDER

We are about to enter the mind of the business executive. The executive who will be analyzed has a particular problem: he is undergoing a career crisis, feeling his whole career is in jeopardy. He may not know exactly how his career crisis came about. His attempts to resolve his crisis have failed. In his desperation he finally turns to a professional counselor for help.

What does an executive who is caught up in the entanglements of business life look like? What causes him to rise to the top only to lose his emotional footing? And if mastery of his career crisis is delayed sufficiently, what kinds of problems are thereby created? How does an executive successfully resolve his crisis and restore harmony with his corporate environment?

This book is about those men who have moved into arrival stages at the top of big business corporations only to reach a point at which the central values of their lives are threatened. At the moment when they would seem to be best prepared to lead, some of them crack under the stresses of corporate life. They have achieved much, they have much more to offer; however, now they are unable, for one reason or another, to remain intensely and meaningfully engaged in their roles. These men are undergoing a painful, humiliating, degrading experience. Some may destroy themselves. The cases in this book tell of men so shocked and scared to see success slip from their reach that they sought psychological help.

The Case of Mark Whiting *

Mark Whiting's own crisis began when word came to him that he had been passed over in favor of an outsider for the corporation presidency. During the course of several counseling sessions, his interpretation of that crucial day was revealed.

It was a day when he would achieve, he thought, the highest point in his career. The board of directors was meeting, and he felt certain that before they were through, he would be named president of Universal Chemical Corporation. All those years he had spent as a manager in almost every department in marketing and sales, and the last four years as vice-president of marketing, seemed to be coming to a logical conclusion. He went over in his mind, as he had done countless times, the sequence of events and achievements, the careful planning, the long hours of work that had brought him to this point. Who else knew the corporation well enough to energize its sprawling resources to accommodate a swelling competitive market? Few men knew marketing and sales as well as he.

He was commonly credited with many firsts in the chemical industry. For his achievements, he had been elected to numerous important committees in the various chemical industry associations and to the presidency of the American Chemical Manufacturers Association. He traveled extensively, giving lectures and speeches before university and nonacademic audiences. He was a familiar figure in Washington, testifying before the Federal Trade Commission, the Pure Food and Drug Administration, and various other agencies concerned with chemical manufacturing. His home life, religious practices, and community associations were exactly as they should be for an executive who conscientiously attempted to be a man on top of his work and career.

* The cases marked by a single asterisk (*) have been documented by means of a thorough investigation of the leading characters involved in the case. This information was obtained after the executive's career difficulties were the outcome of the case.
 The cases marked by a double asterisk (**) are digested presentations of case histories that have been documented or are being documented.
 Both types of cases are composite profiles in that the author has reported the events, and when the major characters had differences of opinion, he has served as the arbitrator.

Recent events seemed to assure his promotion to the presidency. A rumor had been circulating that his long-range program had been adopted by the board of directors. Only this morning an old friend and colleague had reported a rumor that the board had definitely rejected the manufacturing vice-president's program. Such a report from a creditable source increased his confidence that his program was to become the master strategy for the future growth and development of the corporation. After all, there were only two really good reports before the board, and the elimination of one automatically spelled successful adoption of the other.

On an impulse he called his wife, Helen. As he listened to her congratulations, a vague feeling of apprehension moved over him. This feeling of being threatened from no particular direction and yet from all directions was not new to him. But why should he be experiencing it now? His mind turned to previous attacks of anxiety, and he tried to recall the situations in which they had occurred. Helen's voice brought him back to the present. She wanted to know if he was still there. But his affirmative reply was more to assure himself than his wife.

He rang off and buzzed his secretary to ask if the president had returned to his office from the boardroom. He found that the conference was still in progress. Unable to control his mounting tension, he decided to take a walk to bridge the waiting period. For Mark Whiting, the streets below his office had a special significance. In the course of his spectacular rise to the near top of his corporation, he had walked them many times. He sometimes walked to think over his problems and search for decisions that seemed to elude him in his elaborate office many floors above. The anonymity of the crowded streets was often preferable to his office where the noise and lack of privacy seemed to increase with responsibility.

Today he went into the streets hoping to be distracted by the excessive stimuli of the heavily congested business district—anything to occupy his mind until he was certain that the board had made its decision. Then he would return to be summoned by them and given the mandate of carrying out as president the program he had authored as senior executive of marketing.

But the clamor, the variety shops, and the masses of people did not work their spell this afternoon. He could not rid himself of the growing feeling that something was not quite right with his appraisal of his career possibilities. As this feeling increased, he quickened his steps, and by the time he reached his favorite restaurant he was almost out of breath. Finding his lunch unsatisfactory, Mark went outside again, stopping occasionally to look at various items in the display windows but seeing nothing.

It was no particular impulse that caused him to awaken from his self-chosen anonymity. An overwhelming urge forced him to turn abruptly and run back to his office. It suddenly occurred to him why he could not relieve his tension and apprehension. He needed to be in his office in case the board had need of clarification of any kind. Yes, that was it. He should be there to rectify any minor mistakes that had escaped his attention.

But such was not the reception awaiting Mark Whiting. A telephone in his private office was ringing. He almost crashed through the door to see if it was the phone that was used only for conversation with the president and chairman. That phone was silent. He leisurely hung up his hat and coat and walked to his desk, sat down, and picked up the other phone which was still ringing.

It was the same friend who had reported the favorable rumor earlier in the day, a long-time associate who had been director of public relations for the firm for over thirteen years. He apologized and expressed his sympathy to Mark—without the latter knowing why. Mark finally learned that the board of directors had arranged a press conference to announce that a new president had been appointed, a man from the outside with whom the board had been in contact for several months. In utter disbelief, Mark muttered a few incoherent words, not knowing what possibly could have gone wrong. He sat crouched over in his chair, looking down at his faint image in the top of his well polished mahogany desk.

Mark remained for several hours in a state of shock, moving about in an almost complete daze. The sympathetic remarks of his friends and subordinates, the formal announcement that he was to remain as vice-president of marketing, and the attempt of the retiring president to assure him that his future career was indeed secure in the corporation failed to draw him out.

Mark Whiting, fifty-three years of age, at last staggered out of his office toward the now darkened streets below to catch the next commuter train home.

These events had occurred some five years prior to counseling. As Whiting recalled the day that had been relived so many times before, he gradually opened up to register his indictment of the man who had taken the place he felt should have been his. When he first came for professional counseling he wanted to know what an administrative counselor did. He was told that the counselor helps executives who are apprehensive about performing their assignment. His immediate response was that the counselor should get the new president of Universal Chemical on his couch before the man ruined the firm. He emphasized that he personally, had no problems that wouldn't evaporate if only the president was "straightened out."

When Mr. Gray agreed to become president and chief executive officer, he reserved the right to select his own team. This reservation is quite customary in corporate affairs. If the new executive is to be held responsible for executing a program, he must be free to draw upon the managerial personnel as he sees fit. Usually each executive offers his services, even though he knows that others more familiar to the new executive officer may be entrusted with the critical offices and responsibilities. Whiting did not offer his services. He could not even bring himself to congratulate the new president, a man ten years his junior.

Gray had developed a team of highly trusted and skilled executives in his former firm. He brought three members of this team to Universal Chemical. One was made vice-president in charge of marketing, another executive vice-president, and the third, vice-president in charge of scientific and engineering research. The latter was a formally trained scientist with a Ph.D. It was the first time a man with such training had ever moved as high as vice-president in this corporation. Gray had developed a reputation in the industry for organizing and coordinating scientific research for the purpose of developing future markets.

Whiting's program for the future of the corporation did not take basic research into account. He proposed a more vigorous marketing approach with somewhat more emphasis on applied research.

But the corporation had already pioneered a marketing orientation, and Mark Whiting had perfected the approach to the point where the whole corporation pivoted around marketing. The board, however, had decided that the long-range direction and future of the corporation should now come from basic research.

It was not long before Gray and Whiting clashed. Whiting did not "like an outsider coming in and tinkering with my corporation. How could he possibly know what we need and do not need?" He felt that the board had made a terrible mistake, and everything had to be done to protect the corporation from this alien. With this in mind, he attended the first executive committee meeting only to be told that he had been made general manager of all sales under the direction of the vice-president of marketing. He could keep his title of vice-president, however.

The president did not interfere when Whiting attacked his plan to separate marketing from sales. Mark Whiting was given the whole floor, was encouraged to fully develop his view, and was thus allowed to hang himself by showing how incapable he was of working with the new team. Gray belonged to the new school of management that believed in subtlety. He praised Whiting, recognizing his many fine achievements in the chemical industry and emphasizing how important he was to the new team. Consequently, the clash never really occurred.

This engagement set the tone for the years to come. Whiting always struggled to assert himself but could never find the fighting front. The new executive team did not fire any of the old members; it was merely broadened to include them. Yet the old members were kept from the sensitive areas.

Throughout the development of his career Whiting had strengthened already strong needs to know exactly who was boss, what was right and wrong, and to aggressively determine for himself what should or should not be done if a question was not settled by superior authority. What was wrong with Mr. Gray? Whiting did not believe he was a boss who could win the respect of his subordinates by knowing the job better than anyone else.

During counseling, Mark Whiting revealed another critical day in his developing career crisis. On this day, Whiting realized that he was no longer an important member of the firm. This realization came about when he discovered that the executive committee had been meeting regularly twice a week without him. He could not assimilate this fact. His separation from the heart of the corporation now seemed complete.

During the many years that he climbed the corporate ladder, Whiting wanted to get closer and closer to the center of the corporation. The center to him was the decision-making process that spanned the affairs of the whole corporation and was symbolized by that small group of men who met regularly to help the president with these crucial decisions. His new assignment as general manager of sales, however, took him out into the field again.

It was during one of these trips that a division sales manager let it be known that one of his subordinates had recently been picked to become a staff assistant to the new vice-president of marketing. One of his jobs was to take notes in all formal executive committee meetings, which were held twice weekly by the new president.

Upon hearing this, Whiting sped back to the corporate headquarters. His old friend confirmed that he was no longer a member of the executive group. Whiting had now lost more than the anticipated presidency. He had lost his position on the executive committee, which during the last three years had given him much of his self-respect and self-confidence.

Mark Whiting had not been just another cog in the huge corporate wheel. He had been a vital member of a small group of powerful men who prided themselves on their exclusive concern for the overall welfare of the Universal Chemical Corporation. This executive group jealously guarded their prerogatives. In the past, Whiting had considered himself the central figure in the corporate drama that continually unfolded within the human relationships of the group. He had never really thought of what it might be like if he did not have this secure membership.

Now he felt humiliation and shame that bordered on ignominy. This exclusion from "his" executive group amounted to a personal rejection of himself. This hurt, deep inside, far more than having lost something he really had not yet possessed. He had gone from a secure administrative position in an executive group to a boundary position that was partly administrative but largely managerial. Sales policies were being made by the executive committee under the tutelage of the vice-president of marketing. Whiting's job was managing sales policy, and this became excruciatingly painful, self-humiliating, and disgraceful.

Whiting rebelled by not leaving his office for the field. To him, staying on top of the job meant not leaving the office. If the president was trying to keep him from exerting an influence by sending him out to pasture, he simply would not go into the sales field again. And he did not.

Eight months after the arrival of the new president, Whiting was appointed vice-president of special projects. No one ever criticized him for failures that occurred in the sales field due to his lack of attention. In fact, he was congratulated by old and new members of the executive committee for his promotion. Once again, he could find no fighting front.

He was assigned a bigger and better office with a higher classified secretary. He now had a private toilet, shower, and liquor cabinet—all of the trimmings of a corporate president. But he was powerless. He was given problems, every one of which seemed so fuzzy and vague that he could not come to grips with them. When he appealed to Gray for clarification, he was sent on various trips, first to Europe and then to Japan as a special emissary of the president. An inspection trip, an investigating assignment, a good will mission, whatever it was, he never did much of anything that really tied into the administrative decision-making process. He was never invited to attend executive committee meetings.

Gray, however, always made a point of talking to him at least twice a week over cocktails and lunch. This he did for no one else apparently. Whiting came to enjoy these special occasions with Gray and to look forward to them. One day Gray did not keep his usual "social" engagement. Whiting had another attack of anxiety. He wanted to know what had happened. Now what had he done that was so wrong? The president kept his next appointment for lunch and apologized for being busy earlier. Everything was all right after all.

An alternating pattern of contempt and affection for the authority figure, Gray, eventually caused Whiting to think of himself as being as big as the office he occupied. This rationalization allowed him to believe that he was so important that Gray needed the luncheon sessions with him. He idealized his importance on the basis of this presumed friendship and the status symbols of his finely appointed executive suite. His image of himself became idealized to enhance his own feelings of self-worth.

However, these same factors that buoyed up his spirits also caused him to become depressed. The presence of Gray symbolized his failure. Because he could not attend executive committee meetings, Whiting could not gain respect for Gray's administrative skills and organizational dedication. Gray came chiefly to stand for his separation from the central administrative process of the firm. The unearned status trappings of his private office reinforced the feeling that he was nothing. He alternated between moods of elation and depression, feeling one day big and the next day small. When he felt weak, inadequate, and helpless, he would search for signs to assure himself of his power and support. A favorable nod by a member of the executive team, an invitation to any conference or meeting, an attentive ear here and there became crucial to his state of well-being. But of all the sources that could affirm his importance and status, none was as significant as the president. Failure on the part of Gray to take him into consideration as a special person set him into an acute state of anxiety, and he would once again feel terribly weak and puny.

The Universal Chemical Company grew considerably throughout the five years after Mark Whiting was rejected for the presidency. New faces began to appear in high-level positions. Scientists and engineers began to fan out to occupy many positions in the upper managerial functions. The new general manager of sales was an engineer by training; the new manager of the organic chemical products division was a chemical scientist. Several men directly assisting the vice-president of marketing were scientists or engineers.

The corporation acquired a new direction and character, and with each passing day, Mark Whiting's corporation faded into history. What emerged was an entirely different corporation with many different kinds of people. Many on the old team had retired, some earlier than expected. Occupying an isolated role and position, Whiting lacked information about what was going on around him. As he was a stranger to the new breed of managers, so the corporation was a stranger to him.

Whiting came gradually to disbelieve in the corporation as an object or activity which could justify his continued affection and loyalty. In a final effort to salvage a respectable role for himself, he attempted to find employment elsewhere. For eight months he pursued this goal, only to be rejected because of his age or because he demanded too high a salary for the jobs offered to him.

He had one very fine offer. To accept would mean that he would have to forego pension rights and other privileges with this new firm because of his age. If he left his present firm he would sacrifice the same benefits. The several weeks during which he struggled with this decision were the most agonizing in his life. It was during this critical period that he came to the administrative counselor for help.

Mark Whiting's career crisis centered around his problem of authority. Mark Whiting believed his problem was Gray and that Gray alone could relieve him of it.

What is salient about Mark Whiting's career crisis is that he had a long history of difficulty with figures who carried superior authority and with his own acquisition and exercise of authority. In some of the later counseling sessions, he revealed several of these previous difficulties. They had to do with a particular kind of boss. In each case, the superior was very autocratic in his approach to supervision, usually better educated, and of larger physical stature. Mark Whiting had finished only high school and was relatively small in size, a condition to which he attributed many of his problems.

In a very real sense his aggression tapped experiences that occurred as far back as when he sensed that his small build embarrassed his father, who always wanted a son as strong and powerful as himself. He never really forgot the many times that his father shoved him away from manly activities, such as chopping wood, because he was too small. His father once remarked that the ax weighed more than Mark did. The weight of the ax was infinitesimal in proportion to the weight of this remark upon the development of Mark's self-esteem and self-confidence.

Mark never resolved the question of who he was because the one person who could help him, his father, never allowed him to feel important and worthy. Eventually he was forced to come to grips with this question of self-identity.

Upon further analysis of his past, and with the aid of tests, a pattern of distrust toward authority figures became very evident. These figures symbolized restriction of his aims and deprivation of his needs. Authority figures such as teachers, principals, policemen, or ministers were unconsciously perceived as threats to his security and self-esteem.

During his early career in business Whiting was a salesman, and, as such, could be relatively free to express himself in the field away from the sales manager. Because he was one of the best, he was subsequently given a territory to both manage and work. This called for a close relationship with the sales manager of his division and the responsibility for organizing and controlling twenty salesmen. Whiting was fired from this job within six months.

A brief description of this experience is necessary to show that he could not maintain satisfactory relationships with the division sales manager, nor could he supervise his salesmen. He was an autocratic superior who never allowed his salesmen any opportunity to exercise choice, recommend changes, initiate grievances, or communicate in any way except formally. His relations with superiors consisted of offering a constant supply of grievances, gripes, recommendations, suggestions, and sometimes even edicts.

In his next job as a salesman, he regained the vigor of his previous sales style and once again was picked to be a district sales manager. He was fired about a year and a half later for the same reasons.

He found another sales job, this time with Universal Chemical. A friend encouraged him to enter a Dale Carnegie course. Successful completion of this program seemed to give Whiting more self-confidence in handling people, including his district sales manager. For the first time in his still young career, Mark Whiting decided to aim for the top of the corporation. He won an early promotion to district sales manager and then to division sales manager.

At this point he again ran into a thorny relationship with his boss. Intent upon making a success of himself, he resolved his problem for the first time by not leaving the scene. He decided to defer completely to his superior in every minute way and to insist upon such deference from those below him. However, he still distrusted superiors. He kept free and clear of them when possible, drawing mostly from himself the reasons for his managerial decisions. In addition, he threw himself into his work, setting high goals and efficiently achieving them for his organization. In a matter of ten years he moved to the position of general manager of sales with a bright future. He was now in the arrival stage. Here he began to entertain the expectation of becoming the next president. Because such ambition was logical, given his spectacular rise, he allowed a close identification to occur between himself and the corporation. The corporation, its goals, values, people, and rules, became a part of his personality. To conceive of himself without reference to the corporation had become an impossibility.

Whereas few superiors trusted him explicitly, everyone had come to admire his steadfast loyalty and his dedication to the goals and values of the corporation. In his private and community life he imparted the meaning of the corporation. Everyone who knew Mark Whiting knew of his great love for Universal Chemical. He had become a fine speaker, an active member of some of the more prestigious groups, a dependable family man, but most of all, a Universal Chemical man.

When he was promoted to vice-president in charge of both sales and marketing, he enlisted the active support and assistance of a marketing man who had some years earlier tangled with the president. When news of this appointment reached the president, he called Whiting in to inform him of the new appointee's inadequate skill and disloyalty. Whiting took this suggestion as an intrusion into his administrative responsibility, a reflection upon his own competency. He scoffed at the whole affair. He pointed out that few were more loyal than he, and he thus was in a position to see loyalty in others. This remark brought the president to his feet. "Are you, sir, suggesting that I am less loyal than you are?" Whiting retaliated with the point that loyalty to the corporation meant to him that petty past grievances with a subordinate should not stand in the way of seeing and utilizing the latter's competency. Whereupon the president moved out from behind his desk to confront the accuser directly. "Are you, sir, suggesting that I don't know incompetency when I see it?" Whiting replied, "You don't if you can't see competency in this new appointee."

After an intensive hour of this mangling of egos, Whiting was ordered to leave the president's office. He left with his mind made up that he would never let any "knuckle-headed German tell him what to do." During the six months that followed, his relations with the president were very strained. Each seemed to be obstructing the other. Neither one was able to defer to the other.

Whiting's sustained hostility and aggressiveness appeared to be fed by something more than the incident with the president. His attitude was largely energized by the unresolved conflicts with the several superiors who had fired him early in his career. Whiting was getting even with them by attempting to destroy the president. The subordinate over whom the clash occurred turned out to be totally incompetent, a fool, and a knave. This fact only made Whiting more hostile toward the president.

The executive committee was soon split, with some members privately favoring Whiting and others the president. But all were publicly deferential to the president—except Whiting. The storm continued unabated for a year. By the middle of the second year, Whiting's indictment of the president included a list of mistakes, miscalculations, and improprieties. The only reason why he was not removed was because everyone, including the board, felt that Whiting was irreplaceable as senior executive of marketing. While everyone below Whiting deferred to him in the strictest sense of the word, Whiting deferred to no one.

Mark Whiting did not thoroughly understand that the president had more to say about the choice of his successor than any three of the twelve board members. He had made up his mind that Whiting would never become president. He set about on a mission to inform his several close friends on the board of Whiting's limitations as a potential candidate for the presidency. He began to look around both inside and outside of the corporation for a trustworthy replacement. He had vowed that he would retire only when he found someone who could handle Mark Whiting.

Whiting sensed that the president was considering retirement. He also had heard that he was not the most popular candidate with the board. He felt accurately that the president had influenced the board members and that he had to change them in his favor.

He devised a scheme that included submitting to the president and executive committee a long-range program for the future growth and development of Universal Chemical. Since two members of the executive committee besides the president had formal access to board meetings, Whiting was sure the plan would get a hearing with the board of directors. He would be so thorough, clear, and precise in his description of the problems that faced the corporation and how they might be attacked, of the future goals of the corporation and how they would be achieved, that the board would see through the smoke screen laid down by the president.

To soften his aggressive effort, Whiting encouraged the manufacturing vice-president to submit a plan for consideration too. This tactic was aimed at achieving two results: one, to show that Whiting was really interested in the corporation and in getting the best ideas to the board; two, he knew the board would reject the manufacturing vice-president's program. Whiting had sized up his colleague's plan accurately. It was less thorough, clear, and precise than Whiting's. It was rejected, as was Whiting's, but for reasons that Whiting did not understand until halfway through his counseling sessions. Both plans were rejected because the president had made up his mind about his successor.

Gray had already been given a contract with the corporation to become its next president. In one of the interviews, Gray sold the board on his belief that the future of the chemical industry depended upon long-range basic research. The two programs submitted by the manufacturing and marketing vice-presidents were given to Gray for his opinion. He showed how these two men would be useful to him but could not remain in their present roles. Whiting's program had the effect of giving Gray sufficient information about what men to take along with him when his transfer was made complete.

However, he made a gratuitous commitment. He promised that no senior executive would be fired. Whiting's several remaining friends on the board were disarmed by this suggestion and gratefully requested that his offer be read into the minutes of the meeting. Mark Whiting would never be fired.

Actually, Gray was not giving up anything. He really believed before he entered the corporation presidency that Whiting could serve as a liaison officer between scientific research and marketing. He had hoped to appoint him to this position, but such plans were dropped when he discovered that Whiting could not work in such a fluid situation as coordinator. Whiting was so organized emotionally that he had to have firm lines of authority and responsibility. Very early in his relationship with Whiting, Gray decided to shift Whiting to general manager of sales rather than coordinator of research and marketing activities.

The fact that his judgment was accurate was a tribute to Gray's ability to judge people. But it spelled an ominous future for Mark Whiting. The more Whiting showed anxiety, the more Gray relieved him of important work. The more Whiting fed off of his kindnesses, the more Gray was concerned that Whiting was sick. Then Gray made an even greater effort to hold his hand and soothe his ruffled feathers. Soon Gray was privately devoted to Whiting as his special charity. He stood up for Whiting, defended him, encouraged others to go out of their way to be kind to him. Gray strained the resources of the corporation to relieve Whiting's growing anxiety. Whiting was more of a corporate patient than a subordinate. When he became extremely anxious, he would go to Gray, hating himself for it later.

Mark Whiting has never fully recovered from his career crisis. Few do who delay too long the mastery of anxiety. Counseling helped him to see that the problem was as much a part of Mark Whiting as the situation which he faced; that he could not appreciably change the situation confronting him until he changed his notions of who he is and what he wants to become. His career crisis caused him to examine what things in life were worthwhile to him. Such an examination helped him to give up his tenacious hold on the presidency as the highest and only form of self-validation. As this hold relaxed, he looked elsewhere for sources of self-realization, satisfaction, and respect. He now wants to become a useful person in his corporation, community, and society. Consequently, the presidency no longer represents his only form of self-justification.

At first he clung to the roles outside the corporation, much as a drowning man clings to a rescuer. He worked hard in community and national organizations to become useful and constructive. With each little success, Mark Whiting grew more confident and ranged further and wider into his community and society in search of meaningful roles.

One day he discovered that he was actually enjoying these positions. He found himself reordering his whole life around actively advising or directing organizations that ranged from charity to education, religion, and politics. His frequent public appearances and speeches brought much favorable publicity to the corporation. Various members of the board of directors asked him to make speeches for them in their home towns before their business and charitable organizations. Mr. Gray came to believe that Mark Whiting was the best "soft seller" of the social responsibility theme of the business corporation that the chemical industry had. He remarked many times that there were not enough Mark Whitings in America who could effectively get the message across to the people that the large business corporation is not just some economic machine turning out profits to the exclusion of moral and social responsibility.

When Whiting presented a proposal to him that Universal Chemical Corporation contribute to a fund that advanced the educational resources of a consortium of three private colleges, Gray sponsored it before the board of directors. The board ratified an annual contribution of three quarters of a million dollars. Whiting was selected by the consortium to be on its executive committee. He was later elected chairman and executive officer.

It is apparent that Mark Whiting is achieving his goal of finding useful, meaningful roles in his corporation, community, and society. However, periodically he catches himself moving aggressively against some authority figure who makes him feel that he is trespassing or his efforts are unworthy. To this day, Whiting has an occasional recurrence of anxiety, but he now has the ability to bounce back and prove his usefulness through positive administrative achievements.

As a man approaching sixty, Whiting is carving out a useful role for himself. He has lowered his estimate of self, obtained insight into his authority problems, and found other roles outside the corporation to which he may become dedicated. His level of anxiety has become reduced and stabilized, but not completely mastered.

Unfortunately, not all career crises are as favorably resolved as Mark Whiting's. The cases to be reported in this book may seem somewhat disturbing because of the damage often inflicted upon the executive's personality and the destructive forces often directed toward the corporation and other people, including family members and friends.

It is interesting to note that anxiety was believed by the early Greeks to be the disease of their gods. The rulers who today live at the corporation zenith are no less vulnerable to feelings of failure than subordinates below who tend to regard them as more successful.

The Mark Whitings have come to profoundly understand how each successful step forward may increase the threat of failure. When the top rung breaks on the corporate ladder, the executive experiences both success and failure as threatening.

2

THE MAKING OF AN EXECUTIVE

Mark Whiting had an overwhelming urge to achieve his ambitions at all costs. To him success was the measure of the man. Early in his career, as an extraordinarily effective salesman, he expressed this compelling urge to make things happen his way. Gradually his success drive became enmeshed with the corporate hierarchy. He set out with a realistic awareness that he must succeed within the framework prescribed by the corporation's goals, policies, and procedures, and by the special expectations of each authority figure.

Mark Whiting had a pervasive fear of failure. With each step upward, this fear gathered strength. In his more private moments or in the middle of major administrative decisions, his mind would become flooded with a feeling that he might not really succeed and be able to do the things he wanted. Such thoughts mobilized his energy more efficiently to perform his tasks.

He arrived at the post of vice-president almost out of breath because of the pell-mell rush up the corporate ladder. He privately congratulated himself on his ability to succeed, and reassured himself that failure was not in the cards after all. His fantastic success pattern somewhat anesthetized his fears of failure. He had left behind many superiors and subordinates and was not prepared to let anyone block his final bid for success. In this last step upward he placed the total resources of his self.

Mark Whiting's career plans illustrate the central importance of the big business corporation in the minds of executives. Their corporations are relied upon to provide the necessary resources for their personal growth and development. Mark Whiting believed that men at the top had to be big and powerful figures in order to master their giant organizations. To him, movement upward signaled growing and becoming an important and influential person not only in his corporation but in his community and society. The American dream of success was real to him until his career crisis activated the terror of failure.

For the executive, the American dream offers both triumph and terror. Success has a strong kinship to failure. Successful executives are more than high achievers; many, if not most, are chronically fearful of failure. It is common to regard the big business corporation as heir to the vigorous assertion of the success drive. However, the big business corporation causes and is caused by human fear and anxiety. It affirms the central values of success through achievement and satisfaction gained from the secondary rewards of money, status, power, and security. It also tends to reject those individuals who cannot achieve in their work the goals and values of the corporation and the blessings of their superiors.

Success breeds fear and anxiety partly because it is so precariously based upon the expectations and demands of others equally human as one's self. Often these expectations and demands do not rationally fit the corporation's goals and purposes. Many hurts and inconveniences have been inflicted upon subordinates in the name of corporate efficiency and welfare. The irrational needs, whims, and fancies of superiors may be as crucial to career success and failure as the requirements of corporate efficiency and welfare.

The executive knows that successful achievement of the goals and values of the corporation as represented in his job situation may spell failure without the blessings and support of superiors. He also knows that successful achievements of an immediate superior's peculiar expectations and demands may spell failure, owing to the possibility that an even higher superior may indict both subordinates for disregarding the objective necessities of organization efficiency and success. Of course, the individual who acts without regard to either the objectives of the corporation or the expectations of superiors is headed for defeat. The successful executive knows that success presents opportunities for failure. In his inner world, success is closely linked to failure.

often want to keep their technical expertise. They become anxious at making the required separations and attachments.

Thirdly, anxiety becomes involved when attempting to meet the requirements of administration as opposed to management. Activity in the middle and upper-middle ranks is essentially operational. It is concerned with the setting of specific suborganizational goals within the confines of overall policy directives from above. Activity at the top is concerned with developing overall corporate strategy and designing organized structures to achieve the goals and purposes of the firm. It concerns appraising and evaluating corporate achievement. Here the operating orientation of the manager must be left behind and the strategical, evaluative, long-range concern of administration must be acquired. Separation from the former orientation and attachment to the administrative orientation often proves difficult.

For many the movement up into the executive group amounts to an emotional transition. Devising corporate strategy and designing organizational structures and processes to achieve long-range goals calls for distinctly different kinds of emotions than those required in operating a division of the corporation within the constraints determined by top administration. Practically all executives experience some kind of entrance anxiety when they are formally given the more exclusive rights and higher privileges of membership in the executive group. This is the culmination of many years of sacrifice and hope.

The Pull of the Executive Group

In the analysis of the executive career crisis patterns, it is this executive group at the top, rather than the presidency, that is more likely to be the most real and tangible object of middle-managerial ambitions. Membership in this exclusive group constitutes one of the most powerful symbols of achievement, status, power, and money. The overriding motive for belonging, however, is found in the opportunity to become intimately involved in the central administrative process of the firm. This is the symbolic value of the executive group.

The activities of the executive group are associated with the total character and direction of the corporation. One can get no closer to the heart of the corporation and to the central challenges of administrative achievement. It is notable in the case history of Mark Whiting how actively he strove to become a member of this exclusive group, and how separation from it was more painful than the loss of the presidency. The power that membership in this group exercises over people both in and out of it cannot be minimized.

The majority of executives have a high need to achieve. The set of drives to acquire money, power, security, and status is secondary. The high achievers at the lower levels show in their career patterns a constant struggle to get closer and closer to the central administrative processes of the firm. At middle-managerial levels this drive to become intimately attached to the central administrative process acquires added energy and direction. Success has been tasted, confidence won, and the dream of triumphant entry into the executive group is no longer distant. For many it has become a reality. Arrestment of upward mobility is tantamount to separation from the central administrative process of the firm. Success and mobility are clearly perceived to be related to achievement.

The executive group holds out great symbolic value for the minority, who are primarily motivated by a drive for power and affiliation. When the executive with a high need for either achievement or power is finally admitted to the executive group, his orientation gradually changes. The opportunity of greater achievement inherent in the presidency may then become the object for many, and the power and status of the presidency the object for some. Whereas failure to be admitted eventually into the executive group is a great source of anxiety for the ambitious middle manager, failure to become president may produce equal anxiety for an established member of the executive group. But the overriding anxiety in both groups is the apprehension of having their movement toward the central administrative process thwarted or blocked. Getting into the executive group and staying attached to the administrative process is the dominant value of both the high achiever and high power driver. In each case, the executive group holds the key to success.

The executive group is composed of a small number of individuals who come together in face to face groupings to determine and fulfill the task of administering the overall long-range activities of the corporation. Frequent interaction within the executive group produces a feeling of sharing and cohesion. The executive identifies with the corporation and the authority system via this group. It becomes an emotional object, charged with values that lie central to the self.

The executive may attempt to guide his conduct in a deliberate effort to maintain membership in the executive group and, at the same time, an acceptable view of himself. This executive is no automaton. The typical executive has strong notions of self that are forged out of the difficult and intimate associations in the middle-management levels. He carries these notions of self, by which he expects to fulfill their promises, into the executive group.

Here he finds two basic problems. He must take a place among others in the executive group. The group has certain expectations about what is appropriate or valid for him in his position. If he develops behavior patterns which the group regards as invalid for him, he is perceived as marginal or alien. The executive tends to adopt initially a role that the group is most likely to validate.

Role validation is only one problem encountered upon entrance into the executive group. A second problem is role commitment. The two roles are complementary. In the latter, the executive adopts certain styles of behavior that more or less reflect the kind of person he is and wishes to become. He commits himself to a role that will preserve his notions of self and give them productive expression.

The executive enters a transactional process of engineering a role in the executive group which will become validated by them, and to which he may become committed. The group validates roles that fit its functional needs of administration; the executive presents himself in ways that express his personal sense of identity and continuity. The engineering is concluded when the executive arrives at a satisfactory definition of himself validated by the groups' acceptance of his role and style. This process, whereby the negotiation produces role validation by the group and commitment by the person, is sometimes lengthy and exhaustive of emotional resources.

The Making of an Executive

Individuals with strong notions of self and clearly developed capacities for group activity make the adjustment.

The ideal result is that the executive has a secure position in the executive group with an identity that he finds acceptable and worthy. Not only does he function close to the administrative activity of the corporation, he also feels close. His notions of self are allowed to become fused with the central processes of the firm. Acceptance by the executive group brings closeness to the firm.

Likewise, rejection brings alienation from the firm. Not everyone can achieve this ideal adjustment. Some always feel a little detached and anxious. This psychological detachment from the firm, created by low acceptance in the executive group, need not be related to an individual's position in the hierarchy. A president may feel that his executive group has not really accepted him. When this is the case, clinical experience suggests that this president may not feel intimately attached to the corporation as a whole.

Today the executive group is a powerful psychological entity, capable of making people inside and out of it feel important, marginal, or separated. This includes the president. In the case of Mark Whiting, the former president fought Whiting for a number of reasons, not the least of which was his desire to have a clear and unmediated relationship to his executive group. Whiting attempted to come between him and his team. The president made up his mind that Whiting would never again be on the executive team.

Why Executives Keep an Eye on Themselves

The splendors of success and the hazards of failure confront every mobile executive. The rewards must not inflate him and the rebuffs must not intimidate him. To adroitly maneuver among these malevolent forces of the executive's world, he must anchor himself securely to some firm base. In the mobile world of the big business executive, there are few fixed objects. The uncertainties cause mobile executives to seek within themselves a basis of stability. The executive's gyroscope is his sense of identity or self. The terms "self" or "identity" refer to the executive's notions of who he is and what he wants to become.

Examples of success and failure are always present to distract the executive from his work tasks. All around him men move up and down to force continued confrontation of his own possibilities and limitations. The question of who he is and what he wants to become cannot be avoided or easily resolved. But unless the executive can decipher in his early career the basic ingredients of his identity, he has no stabilizing influence by which to assess the value and the costs that success and failure may bring. A strong sense of identity is required to focus upwards and to commence the lengthy, arduous climb. The attempt to achieve mobility is the attempt to maintain and enhance a sense of identity. Success tends to affirm self-notions and failure tends to challenge them.

Notions of self are powerful forces in the human personality. Men will do almost anything to preserve their notions of self-respect and self-worth. Acts of success and failure are capable of helping the individual to realistically appraise and evaluate his notions of self. However, failure is not eagerly sought because of its potential damage to feelings of self-esteem and worth. For this reason, the mobile executive's notions of self become anchored predominantly around his accomplishments. With one hand he points with pride to what he has done and with the other he points with confidence to where he is going. His less praiseworthy deeds are seldom assimilated meaningfully to challenge his emerging notions of self. If he has arrived at the top with few blemishes, he is likely to be overly self-confident. If his climb has been swift, he is apt to have inflated notions of self.

A silent but lethal vulnerability inheres in a rapid, unblemished mobility pattern. It is the lack of skills to cope with self-defeat. It must be assumed that mastering the consequences of success is a product of learning. The same is true for failure. When failure is experienced productively, it provides tools and skills for coping with future defeat. Without the experience of failure, one lacks the means to swiftly and effectively resolve a career crisis. If the executive has made a few mistakes in his career but has not assimilated them, the result may be the same. A career crisis may cause the executive to overreact. He may protest vigorously and aggressively to maintain his acquired notions of self or he may allow his defeat to erode his feelings of self-respect and worth. He may come charging forth against his accusers and opponents or he may withdraw and lick his wounds in obscurity. Aggression and withdrawal will delay the mastering of his career crisis and they may actually cause graver mistakes than those that set off the career crisis.

The executive's view of himself is his most crucial tool for developing and maintaining a productive and satisfying administrative career. When threatened, his career may suffer a partial or complete setback. The search for an adequate executive identity is a central value, and when this search is restricted, such as under conditions of acute threat, the executive's upward mobility is hindered, if not jeopardized. To regain feelings of upward mobility, the executive must once again conduct this search with the resources available to him. He must tap openly and productively the broad range of personality resources at a time when it is most difficult to search for and tap his resources. Few people are equipped to draw back from a conflicting situation and gain distance at the same time. Yet it must be done somehow and to some degree if one is not to be continually overwhelmed at each point of crisis.

Mark Whiting had been able to make the necessary attachments and separations from jobs and men during his rise to the position of vice-president of marketing for the Universal Chemical Company. As vice-president he became closely attached to the values and goals of the corporation. Some of these he had been instrumental in initiating and executing. The bond between his personal identity and his corporate achievements became strong and complete. Whiting conceived of himself as Mr. Universal Chemical Company. This strong attachment between self and corporation eventually prevented him from deferring to the judgment of his superiors.

He had experienced difficulties with authority figures in the past. Anyone who made him feel puny and weak became a threat to his feelings of self-esteem and confidence. As a young man he was aggressive and cocky to compensate for his feelings of inadequacy and inferiority. In his early business career he continued to lash out at those superiors who tended to make him feel weak and small. In order to move up the corporate ladder, Whiting had learned to quash these aggressive feelings under the mask of a deferential attitude toward superiors.

As he moved up the corporate ladder his self-confidence became disproportionately greater. As vice-president of marketing, he allowed his rapid ascent and his many achievements in the executive group to go to his head. He acquired inflated ideas of who he was, what he could do, and where he was going. In other words, he acquired an idealized notion of self. When he was severely reprimanded by the president for his selection of an incompetent subordinate, his enlarged and exaggerated idea of self responded automatically.

His previous pattern of lashing out at superiors who threatened his self-esteem and respect returned in full force. In the period that followed, Whiting nullified all of the accomplishments that he had so carefully achieved for his career's success. He mobilized his forces to prove that he was a bigger, better man than the president who had made him out to be a fool.

The president, however, brought in a successor who inherited all of Whiting's aggressions. Because he had become untrustworthy, unstable, and vindictive, Mr. Gray found it necessary to immobilize Whiting's power and support. His collapse was made complete when the new team finally took away "his" corporation by making it into something entirely different. He was now without an emotional attachment to the corporation and without administrative support from the authority set. His loss of self-respect and confidence made his career crisis complete.

The Need for Autonomy and Integrity

What the executive needs most in a career crisis is autonomy and integrity. Autonomy refers to the capacity to act upon cues derived largely from within. The American stereotype of the autonomous individual is particularly relevant. He is one who has his feet solidly placed on the ground, knows what he wants, and looks forward to achieving it. It is of interest to note that almost all concepts of mental health regard as important the notion that an individual should be able to stand on his own feet without making undue demands and impositions on others. However, the notion of independence suggests an inner freedom that allows the possibility

The Making of an Executive

of choice and decision. Basic to this well-accepted American stereotype is the prior idea that each human being is a unique and separate self. Maintenance and advancement of this uniqueness through freedom of choice is the process of gaining autonomy.

The capacity for autonomy greatly facilitates corporate life. Because the individual feels able to exert some control over his destiny, he is capable of entering voluntarily into organized life and making responsible decisions for others. By his own freedoms and choices, the autonomous executive can apply the rules of authority and organization. He is capable of conforming to the requirements and rules of his superiors and remains free to choose whether to conform or not. In executive language, this eventually means that he is not entirely a creature of his corporate circumstances. More precisely, it means that he applies a personalized style to problems of authority and organization and, thus, creates the necessary conditions of self-realization and acceptance.

Men of the autonomous type have the capacity to make changes that become legitimatized by authority figures and benefit the corporation as a whole. Instead of feeling separated they feel attached. Rather than feeling helpless they feel a commanding sense of effectiveness and power. They both accept the necessities of authority and organization and effect extension of the latter. The autonomous executive feels most acutely the advantages of being involved in the central administrative processes of the firm. He utilizes these advantages to creatively change the corporation. His autonomy allows him to become one independent center of power and influence.

The second characteristic an executive must possess during a career crisis is integrity, or the capacity to maintain a sense of wholeness or unity. This is a most critical resource in times of crisis and is most vividly seen in times of humiliating defeat. The essence of integrity is the ability to remain the same person and to act in line with one's character. The opposite is to fall apart and to lose the normal strengths and recovery powers of the personality through disorganization.

Inherent in every career crisis is the challenge to an executive's integrity. In this sense, a career crisis is not simply a reflection of the errors made by the executive; and it is more than a test of the executive's notions of self. A career crisis is a test of the executive's capacity to remain unified under pressure of disintegration. A stable, realistic set of self-assumptions and beliefs serves as a kind of gyroscope that keeps the ship on an even keel to pursue a steady course toward a predetermined destination.

To observe an executive with this quality of integrity is a rare and delightful experience. It is like seeing a finely honed instrument put to work under the most delicate of conditions. It is much as though the executive comes to life at the point of crisis, having laid dormant in prior periods of tranquility. He seems to be in his elements, to have purposely prepared himself for this very moment. In a way he has, for his prior experiences reflect the learning of the necessary facilities for the mastery of stress. He is a man with the essential inner controls to hold himself together while under a barrage of criticism, degradation, and blame.

When present in the executive's personality, autonomy and integrity reinforce each other during a crisis. They allow for the freedom to make real choices and to draw upon the organized resources of one's personality. Without these two traits the executive in the throes of a career becomes overly excited, loses objectivity, shrinks his capacity to be aware and to take account of reality, formulates faulty assumptions about the causes of his defeat, calls forth alien or undeveloped means of coping, and shows preoccupation with final solutions. If he has a sufficient amount of integrity, he has the capacity to be sufficiently detached, reserved, objective, analytical, and realistic. To some, the executive with autonomy and integrity may appear cold, indifferent, and overly controlled. He appears to fear no one and to blame no one. His main concern is to carry on with little arrestment of his career. He approaches his career difficulty as a problem to be solved and proceeds to construct a strategy to this end. He musters the necessary forces from within and strives to surmount or reverse the negative conditions. His failure is countermanded by his success, and from both experiences he acquires new and improved self-descriptions. He knows more certainly what he can and cannot do, and from this insight he can make more realistic projections of himself into the future. By this process he becomes stronger as a result of his career crisis.

What Whiting Lacked

Whiting lacked both autonomy and integrity. Although he wanted them desperately, he did not know how to get them. His childhood had ill equipped him with the capacity to accept freely and voluntarily the rules of authority and organization. He rebelled at the rightful function of authority. When he deferred to superior authority he did so with the idea of capturing it. If he captured all of the superior authority, there could be none left about which to feel apprehensive and fearful. As it turned out, he had to succumb to the dictates of superior authority or be washed into oblivion.

In the middle-management phase of his career cycle, he developed deferential attitudes out of fear rather than from a rational appreciation of the legitimate role of authority. He was compelled by the force of painful anxiety to subordinate self to superior figures. In the process, he secretly concluded that he was much better than they. Thus started his tendency to idealize his notions of self-importance.

He did not affirm the corporation's goals and values out of choice, but out of a compulsion to get the better of his superiors. Later, he began to innovate changes in the goals and values of the corporation. He performed these maneuvers grandly, in the sense that his changes were validated by the superiors in charge. Because he worked so aggressively for the corporation's goals and values and their improvement, he was promoted over the heads of those superiors who had encouraged him. All the while, he was secretly destroying them by succeeding them. We can see that there is certainly little genuine autonomy in the emotional makeup of Mark Whiting.

By the time he was in his early fifties and in the arrival stage, Mark Whiting believed that he could become president by this same mechanism. He would aggressively work to plan the reordering of the basic posture of the corporation and then seek the approval of the authority set to make him the president. Mark Whiting revealed, in his counseling situation, that he had planned to then remove the old board of directors and eventually have an entirely new one.

Then he was going to get authorization to offer substantial amounts of new stock. The purpose was to broaden the stockholders' base and to make him autonomous from them. Of course, this would be done behind the smoke screen of some logical corporate objective. Ultimately, he would have no one to defer to simply because he had all the authority. He said, "Then I would become free finally to make of my life what I pleased." In this statement we can see a man who believed that he could not be autonomous unless he was without the restraints of superior authority. Obviously, if every executive felt this way, the corporative world would be filled with an unending series of revolutions. No semblance of corporateness would exist.

The corporate organization is perpetuated because there is a sufficient number of executives who conform to the requirements of authority and organization. They have resolved the problems of conformity or rebelliousness in their earlier years. Because they believe in the moral rightness of authority and the imperatives of organized effort, they can make choices that bring a strong sense of self-realization and satisfaction.

Whiting never confronted the conflicts that occurred in his early thirties as an ineffective sales manager. Rather, he denied that these conflicts ever existed. When asked to explain why he moved around a lot, he replied that he was trying to better himself. After many counseling hours, he finally admitted the number of times he had been fired, including instances in his high school years. Whiting revealed how he would aggressively thrust himself into his work as a way to forget about his problems with authority and to allay his anxiety.

The Whiting case illustrates how the fear of success and failure may lurk behind the administrative scenes to influence the way corporations are run and changed. In several of the cases to be presented later, we shall see what happens when a man with administrative anxiety becomes the president, as Mark Whiting almost did. The anxiety-producing forces within the corporation are not to be minimized. The number of men like Mark Whiting, who arrive with bandaged, unhealed wounds incurred in the tense war between self-discovery and realization, and corporation acceptance and validation, is not known.

However, if the executive arrives at the top without having

adequately resolved these crucial problems, he may be forced by extreme circumstances to address himself to their resolution. In a way, the arrival stage is the last opportunity in his career cycle to resolve such fundamental issues. He must decide who he is and what he wants to become, and evaluate the role that authority figures and positions, and corporation goals and achievements, will play in helping him to attain the success that affirms his self-identity.

In this sense, a career crisis may be viewed as therapeutic. It is a kind of shakedown cruise that enables the executive to safely continue his journey toward self-realization. Having successfully mastered a career crisis, few executives wish to undergo another. It has been the experience of the author to note that most are left with a mild fear of career crisis. Whiting still gets occasional pangs of anxiety about how to perform his various administrative roles.

The case of Mark Whiting is not completely resolved. It may seem fantastic to the reader that Whiting has not given up his aim and ambition to become once again an important person in the Universal Chemical Company. In spite of his rebuffs and humiliations, he refuses to believe that his career there is finished. Indefatigable stamina and determination often emerge from executives who are in a career crisis. Executives like Mark Whiting are driven by the need to be successful. Success, when achieved, creates the anxiety of possible failure. And failure refuels the inner fire of success.

3

I WOULD RATHER BE DEAD
THAN A FAILURE

The purpose of a ladder is to aid in reaching inaccessible heights. The corporate zenith qualifies eminently for the use of a ladder. The top positions are presumably out of reach to men without a ladder and without the skills and strengths that are developed by ladder exercises. The corporate ladder transports men to the top, and if they cannot attain sure footing, it helps them back down to more comfortable heights without falling and getting seriously hurt.

Implicit in the character of a corporate ladder is graduated stress. Mastery of small increments of stress develops skills, drive, and confidence that prepare the climber for the next rung of challenges. It is possible to ascend too fast and fail to achieve or reinforce the necessary qualifications, and it is possible to climb too slowly and run out of enthusiasm and initiative. Then, too, the ladder itself may suffer from defects that cause men to trip and hang on precariously until sure footing is regained. Some may start their ascent again; others may become paralyzed midway and give up the climb altogether. A few fall all the way to the ground. Lastly, the ladder may not be long enough to reach the rarified heights of the corporate zenith. This last possibility is worthy of examination. In practice, a short ladder is representative of a corporation that is growing and changing faster than the men who attempt to scale her. The corporation becomes out of reach for the men on the top rung. This may occur because of bewildering changes about which they have little or no awareness and control. Hence, they lack the necessary skills and confidence to manage effectively.

A manager makes things happen according to his design. To do so, he must come to grips with the events and happenings which, if left alone, would nullify his ability to execute his design. He must also order new events and situations rather than be ordered by them. The corporate ladder should produce men capable of taking charge of the corporate situation. Being a product of human contrivance, the corporate ladder occasionally fails to produce take-charge men. Instead, it produces men who react to, rather than initiate, corporate events. These men may become bowled over and dissipate their energies and those of the corporation trying to stave off utter chaos. Their posture is remedial rather than preventive. The latter posture requires a preconceived corporate design that acknowledges known and reoccurring events and situations and leaves margins for unanticipated forces and conditions. The reactor type has no effective design, for if he had, he would be ahead leading the corporate situation rather than following it. Needless to say, innocent and responsible members alike are hurt when men follow a corporation rather than lead it. When a corporation runs out of control, someone usually runs out of a career, so to speak.

A career crisis may be precipitated by changing events and circumstances that call for talent not produced during the climb to the top. During the last decade and a half the economy has almost doubled its gross national product. With this growth have occurred rapid technological, scientific, social, and political changes in the internal and external environments of the large business corporation. These changes have not left the art and science of management intact. Men with vision and a flair for innovation have reached out to utilize new tools and concepts to cope with changes and problems inside and outside of the corporation. They have gained thereby a measure of mastery that otherwise would not have been possible. These managers have grown and by their growth they have enhanced change and development of the economy as a whole. They know that change is required to master change.

Other executives assumed a different posture during this period of unheralded growth and prosperity. The swirling events and happenings tended to confuse and frighten them. With their footings made precarious and unsure, they turned back and grabbed hold of the ladder lest they fall down. In practice these managers became rigid in their state of near panic. They relied too heavily upon set patterns of management. In effect, what they had learned on the rung below seemed good enough for the discharging of presidential responsibilities. They assumed that these gyrations at the top could be overruled by guts and convention. Did not the lengthy, exhausting climb to the top prepare them as well as possible? If they were not prepared now, they would never be prepared. In a mixed state of near fright and naive confidence they attempted to force things to happen as they intended. But they had no design, no strategy that was born of real insight and understanding. They tried more or less to superimpose a conventional, rigid, authoritarian management style upon the changing events and situations. Events of the last decade and a half, however, proved to be far too illusive and unpredictable for their rigid, coercive techniques.

During this period of great prosperity, many managers failed and some failed miserably. Their corporations exceeded their reaches, and without something to span the distance, they fell with a thud to the ground below. It was common for them to fall and not regain full consciousness for some time after. For days, weeks, and sometimes months, they aimlessly and unsteadily walked around without the benefit of full awareness and understanding about what happened to them. When the shock subsided and their faculties returned fully, they often spun convenient myths that served two purposes. Their rationalizations helped to blame others and relieve them of all personal responsibility, and to propel them back into action. Having learned little from their fall, they often repeated their mistakes and fell a second time. With both their careers and corporations beyond their power of management, they fell into an abyss of depression and apathy or hatred and vindictiveness. Having reached rock bottom and their fondest dreams shattered, a few rolled over and, face down, gave up. Others found within themselves emergency powers of recovery that come to men only when they are faced with total extinction. The case of Will Fowler is representative of a large number of executives who failed during the period of growth and prosperity.

The Case of Will Fowler *

Will Fowler's own crisis began when he stepped off the elevator and met his vice-president in charge of marketing, Paul D. Gage. Will asked why Paul was not going to the board of directors meeting. Said Gage, "It's all over, Will. We've had it." In a matter of minutes, Will Fowler's forty-year career, topped off as president and chairman of the board of the giant American Farm Equipment Corporation (AFEC) came to a screeching halt. With a sense of foreboding, Will Fowler entered the heavily draped, dark panelled boardroom. His chair at the head of a long egg-shaped walnut table was occupied by a stranger. Before he left this room, Will Fowler reluctantly added his resignation to a large number already submitted. The corporation was taken over by a group of investors. Their concern for American Farm Equipment Corporation's future started with the removal of what they called "a small group of smug, authoritarian, and closed mind" executive officers. Will Fowler headed this cast of "primitive managers."

An hour after entering the boardroom, Will Fowler returned to the elevator and did not stop at his office on the floor below. Rather, he went straight home, something he did rarely. For that matter, Will Fowler had never experienced a crisis of this magnitude. His wife, surprised to see him home this early, could read his face well after thirty-five years of marriage. She reasoned that this was no strike at the plant, no discovery of cash shortage, no sudden death of a colleague. There was something fundamentally wrong with Will. He had been cruelly and boorishly hurt. He looked depressed, seemed possessed, became inaccessible. In time she got out of him the complete story, and with it she caught the inexpressible ignominy of his experience in the boardroom.

For several days, Will Fowler was mentally and emotionally paralyzed. He said nothing, did nothing. He never got out of his pajamas and never left the house. A week after his racking nightmare in the boardroom, Will Fowler sent for his personal belongings, and together with his wife left for a cruise in the Bahamas. Two days out of port he suffered a massive cardiac infarction. He was taken in a hastily improvised oxygen tent to the mainland in a U.S. coast guard helicopter. The attending physician feared for his life. He reported to the oldest son that his father had no desire to live. But Will Fowler maintained his precarious hold on life and survived. At age fifty-seven his physical crisis was over, but his career crisis had just begun.

Will Fowler left high school to go to work in a malleable iron foundry owned by American Farm Equipment Corporation. He worked every job—cupola-tapping, moulding, shaking, coring, grinding—and became foreman, foundry superintendent, plant manager, and general manager by the age of thirty. Thereafter his rise to the top was slow but steady. He never received a demotion, never experienced a crisis of his career. The farm manufacturing industry was largely propelled by men of Will Fowler's cast. Hard working and practical, they started at the bottom and acquired the art of farm implement production and management through experience. They cared little for theories, boasted of their lack of formal education, prided themselves on their graduation from the school of hard knocks. Upon achieving the presidency, they assumed that they would remain chief executive officers as long as they could hold the reins and steer the team through the muddy fields of economic competition. They expected to serve out their careers and retire at the mandatory age. Will Fowler had a good ten years to go before his fall off the corporate ladder. At this time he was just beginning to feel the rhythm of the presidency. His confidence was high as was his estimate of self-worth. He looked forward to a decade of high achievement for himself and American Farm Equipment Corporation.

In his steady climb to the corporate zenith, Will Fowler did not see the gradual changes emerging in the managerial world outside his firm and industry. He had mastered the art of management as his tutors had learned it, but he did not keep abreast of the technological and scientific approaches and skills that were eventually to move into the management discipline. Nor did he believe he needed to. Consequently, he did not see that men on the move in higher management were college educated and knew how to use these scientific tools and skills. In 1956, when he was made president, he did not see that he and others of his cast would be replaced soon by the new professional breed of manager.

While recovering from his heart attack, he had time to reflect. He rolled over in his mind the list of charges that comprised the indictment that led to his ouster. Why had he not gone to the stockholders for approval of a modernization program that called for spending a sum equal to half of American's assets? Why had he refused to give to the new investor group information about a planned loan and the names of the insurance companies and banks and other details? Why had he stacked the board of directors with vendor directors who were beholden to him, and with his officers or retired officers who had no choice but to go along with him? Why had he, as chairman of the board, and his executive committee made all decisions and formulated board policy without so much as consulting the other board members? Why had he not trained an executive vice-president and a replacement for himself as the president? Why had he kept in crucial executive positions old cronies who were incapable of delivering high performance?

In short, the indictment pictured Will Fowler as incompetent, autocratic, unscientific, and unprofessional. He was denounced, ridiculed, and held accountable for American's drop in sales from third position to seventh in the industry. AFEC's shares in cash value dropped from about sixty-nine dollars to eighteen in two years. He was scapegoated for the deterioration and disintegration of a great corporation.

Each time Will Fowler moved mentally through this list of charges, he gathered more facts, recalled additional experiences, and reworked old arguments to better justify his defense. By the time that he had sufficiently recovered from his illness, Will Fowler was ready to make his case stick as a victimized, persecuted hero. But in five months time a new top management team had replaced his group and were settled snuggly in their positions. The new board had voted him a pension and approved a retirement program equal to what he would have gotten had he completed his tenure. He could not fight back because they would not listen to him, either because they were indifferent strangers or compassionately inaccessible friends.

Will Fowler's career crisis lasted five years. At midpoint in his crisis he came for professional counseling. He reported that after his recovery from his heart attack, he went from one interview to another, never landing an offer satisfactory to his self-respect and worth. Because his whole life was wrapped up in the farm equipment business, he sought positions with related firms, only to be beaten out by members of the new breed of professional, scientific manager. Finally, he was accepted for the presidency of a small firm which carried a salary of one-fourth his former wage. Swallowing his pride and believing that he could still manage, he accepted this position. Within one year he was summarily removed. The reasons were the same as before—too autocratic, too intuitive, too unprofessional.

This second dismissal turned out to be a therapeutic necessity. He needed to have reenacted the original scene in order to start on a new course of self-discovery and insight. As president he inherited a small staff of senior executives whose positions were made secure by the members of the family that owned the firm. Whereas he deferred to the family members occasionally, he aggressively dictated to this very secure little band of corporate executives. They were accustomed to entering actively into discussions as a kind of corporate family. They were brought up in an essentially warm, friendly, patronizing climate. Will Fowler's cold, rigid, autocratic style moved them to reject him shortly after his arrival. Their rejection caused him to become a bully and to insist that they observe the manners and morals becoming to superiors and subordinates. If he was autocratic when he arrived, he became grossly dictatorial, displaying the airs of a martinet. In time, this small band of uncomfortable subordinates went to the widow of the founding father and pressed their apprehensions and discomforts upon her. She immediately took steps that culminated with the purchasing of the contract of Will Fowler.

As he related these events, Will Fowler gave forth his bitter feelings about what happened when he was invited to be president of American Farm Equipment Corporation. Among the many facets of this weird event, one stands out in his mind as an organizing force contributing to his career crisis. The president, Mr. Hand, died suddenly of a heart attack. The board of directors decided to look carefully at candidates both inside and outside of the corporation. To help them with this responsibility, they hired a large, nationally based, management consulting firm. The consultants studied the men in the corporation first, but found no one who was both physically fit and managerially prepared for the presidency. They included Will Fowler, vice-president of operations, in this category. Unfortunately, he was not on the board or on the selection committee for the new president and did not know of their findings until the consultants proceeded to look outside the company. The search for executive talent cannot be kept a secret very long. Word came back to Will Fowler that the company was looking outside. This meant that he had been rejected. Later, he learned why he had been passed up. One reason was that he was a protégé of the former president. Everything he knew had been taught to him by the former president. He was one of his foremen when the president was plant manager of malleable iron foundry. They had climbed the ladder together. Will Fowler was a crucial subordinate in that he was extremely basic to his superior's effectiveness. It was logical to him and others that he would succeed to the presidency. The president, Mr. Hand, had told several directors privately that he expected some day to nominate Will Fowler to succeed him, but that he needed more time for development. He repeated this statement only a week before he died. At that time he was interpreted as saying that Will Fowler was all but polished. Mr. Hand said, "Will is a sleeping giant whose masterful powers will come to life when given final authority." But the management consultants disagreed. They saw in Will Fowler a man who was good at managerial routines, of limited imagination, poor in his relationships with subordinates, and potentially aggressive in his relationships with superiors. Most importantly, he was without scientific and professional orientation and tools. He seemed absolutely unsuited and unqualified for top management. To appoint Will Fowler was to accept the nineteenth century over the twentieth. The management consultants convinced the board of his weaknesses. They produced two candidates from the outside, both of whom became uninterested after talking to the board. The board appeared split to them. One group wanted a marketing oriented president with secondary competency in finance. The other group wanted a strong manufacturing president with secondary competency in finance. The board agreed on the secondary value of financial skill, and this placed them at odds with the two candidates who took a look at AFEC and concluded independently that finance was the primary problem. However, neither candidate was highly qualified in finance and neither was anxious to give up his present security for a gamble with AFEC. The board was not prepared to go the full route required to give them financial security. The next two candidates from the outside had sound financial backgrounds, but both executives wanted the chairmanship as well as the presidency. They considered this necessary because the financial needs of the corporation would require aggressive policy formulation and close stockholder relationships. The board appeared unwilling to trust a stranger in both positions and turned them down too.

While all of this interviewing and evaluating of candidates was transpiring, Will Fowler was asked to assume the duties of president with the title of acting chief executive officer. As long as nine months after Will Fowler assumed the role of acting president, no eligible candidate had appeared. The word circulated in the stock market that AFEC could not find a president. Trading of the stock became irregular, the price of its stock declined rapidly, rumors circulated that AFEC was in financial trouble. The board recalled their disagreement over Will Fowler and over what the former president had said about him. In desperation, they rationalized his weaknesses, modified the meaning of the dead president's observation, fired the management consultants, and turned to Will Fowler, who was waiting patiently for this turn of events. They summoned him to appear before them and to report on the state of the corporation. In spite of his obvious lack of administrative experience and financial competency, Will Fowler was asked to be president. There was simply no one else to put into the job. He was at the right spot at the right time.

Looking back, Will Fowler realizes that he was miscast. Will became a victim of circumstance. However, at the time he vowed that he would "show them what a president really looked like. I have not come this far to be turned back by men who need consultants to tell them what a president looks like." Coming from manufacturing, he was aware that the corporation needed overhauling. It needed modernization, but to do this he needed money. He launched arbitrarily an ill-conceived modernization and capitalization program and thrust it down the board's throat. At first, the board was unwilling to go along with him, but he called for a vote of confidence and suggested that the board might be expanded to include members from the banking institutions. With the stock market as shaky as it was, he got the vote of confidence and handpicked four new members of the board, two of whom were bankers. The board now comprised twelve, including himself. In private he talked two senior members of the firm into retiring, one of whom was the board chairman, and replaced them with two from his executive staff. He called for nominations for board chairmanship and nominated his best friend, one of the bankers. The other banker friend moved that the nominations be closed, whereupon the nominee rejected the opportunity and nominated Will Fowler. The vote was unanimous. He was now president and board chairman and ready to show the world that he, Will Fowler, knew how to make things happen his way. In the second year of his regime he and his four bankers and two executive subordinates outvoted the other members to enlarge the board to eighteen. He handpicked three new members from a group of vendors and three from his long list of acquaintances. One was a clergyman. After this board enlargement, the few original board members surrendered their power to management. Will Fowler became the supreme authority of the whole corporation. There was no one left to obscure his vision and impede his aims.

Will Fowler failed to take note of a small group of investors who started to buy stock soon after his modernization program was publicly announced. In Will's fourth year as president the small investor group acquired the largest single block of voting stock. Their representative appeared before the board to ask for a seat on the board. In effect, the representative challenged Will Fowler's authority. The board voted down the request. After the request was made unsuccessfully two additional times, the small investor group threatened a proxy battle. Will Fowler lost his grip slightly when his board gave in to the request in order to avoid a proxy fight. Once on the board the investor group got access to the information about the incompetency of the top management. Three months before the annual stockholders meeting, the investor group produced a dossier on Will Fowler, noting his lack of competency, his inadequate, ill-financed modernization program, his vendor directorships, and his poor executive staff. Armed with this damaging evidence, the investor group demanded six seats on the board and the board chairmanship. The struggle between Will Fowler and the investor group lasted two days without conclusive results. But the investor group held the trump card. The annual stockholders meeting was only weeks away. The board of directors could not allow the contents of the dossier to be made known and broadcasted before the unsuspecting stockholders. They feared dire consequences to the corporation, but mostly to themselves. An emergency meeting was called by three board members, two of which were vendor directors. Will Fowler was scheduled back from a trip to Canada in time for the board meeting. His plane was late in arriving because of bad weather. By the time he got to the boardroom, six directors had resigned, including his two vice-presidents, and the new board had voted a new chairman. When Will walked into the boardroom and saw a new chairman, he immediately wanted to know what had happened. When informed of their decision to remove him from the chairmanship but let him remain president, Will Fowler replied in a manner entirely characteristic of him, "If you don't have confidence in me as chairman and chief executive officer, you certainly don't have confidence in me as president. Either I have both or you will have to find another man." He was confident that they could not. He proceeded to inform the board of the difficulty of getting a man well experienced in this business with a solid background in the crucial phases of management. He informed them of his achievements and qualifications and portrayed the investor group as having selfish interests at heart. He had spent his whole adult life in AFEC, and he could be depended upon to sacrifice himself for its future well-being. He prided himself on his frankness, his honesty, his ability to call "a spade a spade." One always knew how one stood with Will Fowler, and he believed that was the way it should be. He said, "We have too many so-called managers who don't manage, who take ten ways to say the same thing and still say nothing. . . . You say that this corporation is sick. I say to you that its foundation is being eaten away by termites, but that once fumigated it will recover its previous strength. I intend to fumigate."

At this point Will Fowler was falling rapidly to the ground. He had knocked the ladder out from underneath him by his impudent, ill-considered, frontal attacks on the powerful investor group. They resolved that he could not be president, let alone chairman. He would simply have to go. Without their help, Will Fowler removed himself from the presidency. While they individually lost what little respect they had for him, Will Fowler got a tremendous surge of confidence and righteousness. He called for a formal vote on his remaining as chairman and president. He lost both. The thud of his crash was rivaled only by the slam of the door as he left the boardroom.

Will Fowler was succeeded by Carl Warner, a man fourteen years his junior, who had a master's degree in business administration, had spent over six hundred hours in management seminars, had been in accounting, sales, and manufacturing, and had spent his three years before coming to AFEC in the internal organization of his former company. But among the many things that differentiated Will Fowler from his successor, one stood out most clearly. Carl Warner viewed his own personal development as a training process. Carl was never too old to learn. To him, managing was the art and science of gaining and creating knowledge. The job of an executive was to develop and utilize people who knew more than he did and could bring this superior knowledge to bear upon the practical problems in the management situation. In the past Carl Warner found that his orientation bred a corporate staff that was open to ideas. Power and authority tended to devolve upon people who had superior ideas and performance. He believed that the objective of the corporation was to know more about the critical phases of farm machine manufacture and sales than competitors. If his corporation had superior wisdom, profits would be a necessary consequence. If the corporation was a creator of knowledge, it had to find knowledgeable people and train and develop them. The climb up the corporate ladder was to be a learning process, a developmental, dynamic experience. Under Carl Warner, the corporation is now recruiting vigorously college graduates, setting up training and development programs for managers, engineers, salesmen, and executives. In this respect Carl Warner is a symbol of the changes that have occurred in the management mix during the last decade.

In 1948 to 1953 ten percent of the presidents of our largest industrial corporations had master's degrees. By 1963 thirty-three percent had advanced degrees, by 1964 thirty-seven percent. It is expected that by 1970 forty-five percent will have master's degrees. Presidents are better educated to begin with and go to many training programs and seminars after they start their climb to the top. In 1948 to 1954 the average president spent about fifty hours in classes of a training or developmental nature inside and outside of the corporation while he was president. From 1960 to 1965 the president spent on the average of five hundred hours in classes between the time he left college and became president.

Executives are coming up younger. In 1948 to 1953 the average age when made president was sixty-one to sixty-three for seventy percent. In 1961 to 1965 the average age when made president for seventy percent was fifty-one to fifty-three. Ten full years were taken off of the age levels. Executives are coming up faster, too. In the 1930's it took twenty-nine to thirty years to build a president once he started his managerial career. In the 1940's and early 1950's the length of time dropped to twenty-five years on the average, and in 1965 the average president had taken nineteen years to go from first-level management to the top. In short, the men coming to the top in our giant organizations are better educated, better trained, younger, and are arriving faster. But most of all, they believe in knowledge, learning, research, science. They believe in utilizing every possible tool or device to make them better aware of the situation in which they manage. In this regard they are openminded, other-directed, and flexible. No doubt this new breed will prove eventually to have its shortcomings. Meanwhile, they are rapidly replacing the Will Fowlers. The corporate ladder is not the same as it was at the start of the midpoint of this century.

Will Fowler thought that he had served his apprenticeship and learned the art of management. "I never figured that with each promotion I had opened a new avenue of learning. I never realized that my assumptions about what makes people tick were obsolete. . . . I did not realize that developing a team of subordinates more talented individually than I, was a managerial responsibility. I had always believed that I knew more than my subordinates or I couldn't have gotten where I am. . . . It never occurred to me that there was more to learn the higher one got to the top. I had the feeling that once I got to the top I had only to use what I had already learned. I didn't realize that I was slowly ossifying the closer I got to the president. I see now that the top job is most difficult because it requires so much to learn."

The Recovery of Will Fowler

In 1964 Will Fowler was fortunate in acquiring a position with a firm in the oil business. His job was corporate advisor to the executive committee of the board of directors. As such, he would advise on reorganization of the corporation that had become bogged down in a myriad of committees and decision-making groups. Because he was a renowned autocrat, he was expected to bring some of this style to the corporation that had moved too far the other way. In the process he learned a lot about how to blend his autocratic style with a more permissive, democratic one. He achieved a blending of the two that he had never before experienced. The corporate reorganization plan was adopted by the board and executed in the fall of 1965. Had Will Fowler sufficient knowledge of this oil industry, he might have become president. Instead, the board asked him to stay on as vice-president in charge of corporate planning and development. He is presently carrying out a respectable position for himself amidst a community of respectful associates. He has a different notion of what constitutes the executive role. He sees better that the objective and goals of large corporations require the blending of men and skills of different orders and strengths. He sees better who he is and now has a better plan for achieving his goals.

In his position as chairman of the corporate planning and development committee, Will Fowler is attempting to make up for past mistakes. He is reading eagerly, going to seminars and conferences, staying abreast of the latest subjects relevant to management, organization, and human enterprise. He is assembling a staff of extremely bright, learned, and capable researchers, advisors, and managers. His planning committee is becoming highly respected for its knowledge of the events and happenings of the industry, of economic, social, political trends, of human behavior. Will Fowler is having the time of his life and is looking forward to having his fondest dream realized.

With each round of success, Will Fowler refuels his desire to become president of a major corporation some day. Whether or not he will, remains to be seen. He certainly feels better prepared than when he assumed the previous two presidencies. He certainly has acquired a new set of credentials. But his most conspicuous quality is an enlarged view of the game of success. He believes that success is a marriage between the man and the times. The qualities of success are situationally relevant. With a detachment uncommon to his previous mode of thinking, he can single out executives who have failed because situational changes during the last decade required men of different talents and orientation. Why did not executives see these changes in time to head off a career defeat? He attributes failure to the nature of the corporate ladder itself. Executives who came for professional counseling during this period of growth and change uniformly bear witness to his explanation. In order to accommodate growth, managers and executives moved up faster than usual. This rapid climb stimulated feelings of competency greater than competency itself. It was much as though success overly reinforced an emerging pattern or style of managing, and rapid success actually forced premature closure. This means that men nearing the top had managerial styles that were incomplete, premature, and too rigid. This rigidity included a skewing of the personality in such a way that established ways of managing became overworked. In such cases, the capacity to be aware of the developing situation and sensitive to significant dangers narrows and atrophies. When this happens, the executive attends to a limited part of the management solution, that which he knows best and feels most comfortable about. Things may appear to be going well for him, but actually he is in trouble.

At this point, one ingredient may cue off career difficulty. It is a superior or authority group that has a more enlarged or radically different view of the situation facing the corporation. Differences between superiors and subordinates about the requirements of the managerial situation may be ironed out if each has retained flexibility. If not, conflict may ensue in overt or subtle forms, or both, and may make the executive even more rigid. Rigidity will grow out of conflict if the executive feels threatened by sustained differences with his superiors. Some executives do not value highly smooth upward relationships simply because they do not value highly continuation of upward mobility. A highly mobile oriented executive may react to conflict out of fear of the consequences to his career. If he does, two noticeable patterns may evolve and we saw these two styles emerge in the wild period of the last decade.

Counseling of executives showed that some panicked and, out of fear, accepted blindly the premises of their superiors. This deferential attitude was not based upon a genuine understanding of these premises but upon a desire to dispel the conflict. Because these premises were not believed and understood, they became mere appendages to the executive's managerial style. They were used to alleviate fear and conflict and were not used to help him perform more productively in his managerial role. The consequence was that the executive commenced to wear a mask. While his mask enhanced cordial relations with his superiors, it had the damaging effect of preserving his basic assumptions and beliefs that made up his managerial style. While he appeared to be a changed man to his superiors, inwardly the ossification process proceeded unabated. At some point in his career crisis, he discovered his two selves. Then a new fear set in. It was the fear that he would be discovered, that his superiors would see his mask, tear it off, and reveal his true identity. The fear of being uncovered is the fear of becoming obsolete. The consequences to his career may be frightening indeed. To prevent discovery the executive worked hard at perfecting his mask. In practice this amounted to becoming everything his superiors wanted him to become. A vicious cycle developed. The more he perfected his assumed identity, the more he became estranged from his real self. When his true beliefs, assumptions, and talents threatened to break out or become discovered, he worked harder to perfect his mask. It was possible for a complete transformation to occur within a few years. But the change was more apparent than real.

Nevertheless, it was possible that the executive's career became enhanced. We shall present a case of an executive, Olaf Johnson (Chapter 6), who developed a mask that made him appear the most likely successor to the president. He succeeded to office only to be unmasked, not by a perceptive superior or subordinate, but by his own failure to come to grips with the crucial requirements of the managerial situation at the corporate top. With no one to tell him, he could not feel secure about his interpretation of the managerial scene. In a state of fright, he attempted to retrieve the elements of his former management style. He returned to his real self. In the period of one year the executive did a flip-flop. His subsequent removal from office sent him into a state of depression that required psychiatric treatment.

Will Fowler was not a conformist in his approach to the presidency of AFEC. He resolved that he would be true to himself. Will Fowler did not assume a false identity to overcome conflict with his superiors. Rather, he decided to overwhelm his opposition with his vast supply of energy, convictions, reputation, achievements, and skills. They would come to defer to him rather than he to them. This pattern was the second alternative that was often discovered in the counseling of executives in career crisis. It was far more common than the pattern of conforming. It was based upon the complete rejection of any false or alien values, concepts, and skills, and upon the total acceptance and affirmation of his true identity.

One may ask, How do we know that Will Fowler is not wearing a mask? This question is legitimate. Will Fowler is certainly a changed man. His style is unlike that which he had so carefully and assiduously developed in his many years with AFEC. This acute transformation occurred in a period of twenty months. Is it possible for a man approaching sixty to change radically? And if he moves to a third presidency, will he revert to his former autocratic style of managing? Although these questions seem appropriate to Will Fowler's case history, they are no longer meaningful to him. He knows what he has been through. He says that he feels secure in his new approach to management. He appears not to be defensive, but he is aware of the fact that his style is still emerging. What will happen if he becomes a corporation president again?

Well, he does not rightly know. For that matter, who really knows what he will become when given the authority and status of chief executive officer. No ladder can reach the top completely. In Will Fowler's words, "There must always be some distance between what a man is prepared and qualified to do and what is required of him. Without this difference, there is no challenge. Without challenge, there is no meaning in climbing the ladder in the first place." If movement from a lower rung to a higher rung were a sure thing, there would be no need for rungs. In that case there would be no failures. Concluded Will Fowler, "I am willing to try again, I must try again. Of course, the movement into the presidency is a leap into the unknown. Some are frightened by the risk and back off. They recline on neatly prepared corporate rungs and are given special problems that do not disturb their precarious balance. Not me, I know who I am and what I am capable of becoming. I shall not rest until I have proved myself. I would rather be dead than a failure."

4

WHAT TO DO
UNTIL THE COUNSELOR COMES

A career crisis is basically a crisis of self. The executive may be a president threatened with overnight expulsion from the corporation, as was the case of Will Fowler. Or he may be in an intensive, protracted battle to achieve full control of the firm, as was the case of Mark Whiting. Whatever the case, a career crisis is to be distinguished from the kinds of crises an executive faces from time to time that are directly related to corporate achievement. These crises may not, at first, directly relate to the career of the executive, but they may eventually affect it.

A career crisis is a situation in which the executive is faced with a decision to act largely and primarily on behalf of self. It may involve staying in the firm and plotting a strategy to alleviate the crisis, or it may involve leaving and starting a career with another firm. Regardless of the alternatives, a decision is necessary. What differentiates a career decision from other kinds of executive decisions is that the executive has foremost in his mind the alleviation of personal difficulty. If he stays with the firm, his decision may appear outwardly very rational and organizationally relevant. In fact, it must be to be effective. It may not differ in objective content from that of any other decision. It must be situationally relevant and administratively proper. Yet, it does not basically ensue from the requirements of the objective situation, but rather the decision emanates from an inner struggle to alleviate pain and discomfort.

For example, a vice-president of marketing in a large electrical manufacturing firm was faced with the distinct possibility of forced early retirement. To counter this move on the part of the chairman of the board, he devised a new strategy for marketing accessory appliance products. He worked vigorously on the plan, mustered scarce and costly personnel to help in its formulation, and carefully laid a groundwork for the plan's eventual adoption. The scheme was basically sound, as its final adoption so testified. However, the executive devised the whole matter as an attempt to ward off an offensive maneuver by the board chairman. Interestingly enough, his career was prolonged by the exact amount of time it took him to see the strategy successfully implemented, which was five years, after which he was better prepared psychologically for retirement.

The distinction between a career decision and a situationally or administratively based decision is indeed tenuous and fine. For the upwardly mobile executive there may not be a distinction. Some believe their decisions are always career oriented. But what if the upwardly mobile executive is faced with expulsion, separation, or rejection? In this case, what makes a career decision different is that a crisis in one's career is subjectively felt, and what is felt becomes the major basis of the decision.

The case of Mark Whiting is instructive at this point. He manufactured a long-range program that outlined the future growth and expansion of the Universal Chemical Corporation. He submitted this plan to the board of directors in an attempt to rebut the president's view that he was incompetent, disloyal, and immature. Whiting attempted to reorder the affairs of a vast corporation to allay his apprehension of immediate and total failure.

The number of corporations that are changed or reorganized by executives to accommodate their inner needs to avoid insecurity and anxiety is indeed difficult to determine. The important point is that the stereotyped image of the rational executive sitting at the center of an impersonal communications network is not always accurate. He may be deploying units of personnel and scarce resources to relieve a subjectively felt, impending career crisis.

After ten years of counseling big business executives through career crises, it has become apparent that their problems seem to involve a personalized definition of what constitutes the task of administration. Men who have had their upward mobility arrested at a very high level in the corporation evolve a mode of thinking that may not have occurred to them during their prior successful stages. When the chips are down, and the future appears bleak and foreboding, the executive needs to perform what would seemingly be an elementary exercise to any administrator. It is not, however. It is difficult for a troubled executive to ask simple questions as to what is the administrative task and what he is doing wrong. To be sure, he has entertained such questions, perhaps often in the past, as an academic exercise in seminars, or in *ad hoc* debate with his colleagues, or as problems brought on by the misconduct of others about him. In fact, it has become quite stylish today, for executives to raise sophisticated questions about the process of administration and the duties and responsibilities of execution.

In this regard, Mark Whiting often lectured to university schools of business about the skills and capacities of an effective administrator, and he acquired quite a following among university faculty and students in various parts of the country. He often started to lecture with a question about what constitutes the real "guts" of managing today. Like Mark Whiting, many business executives are interested in this question as an exercise in academic theorizing.

However, few executives invoke this question as seriously as when undergoing a career crisis. The thought has often occurred to the author that perhaps executives who do not seriously ask these questions prepare themselves, unknowingly, for a career crisis; or perhaps executives who continue their upward mobility do not have to ask these questions. In any case, an executive who is faced with the imminent possibility of being removed or shelved, and who regards this possibility with much distress and anxiety, eventually and invariably questions the very activity in which he has been engaged for the better part of his adult life. But he goes through a song and dance aimed at preserving the notion that other people are his problems, not himself.

The executive in a career crisis does not approach a counselor with naked statements of his emotional distress. He may come out with the fact that the president is trying to get him fired, or a colleague with whom he has had an untold number of clashes and disputes is about to become the boss, or that he cannot really make a big decision when the pressure is on. More often, he comes to an administrative counselor to get help with problems centered in people other than himself, who, however, may have made things very difficult for him. A person earning thirty thousand dollars a year or more is not expected to have many problems more "personal" than these. His administrative difficulties are supposed to be anchored in other people, and their problems are only his by definition of his role as boss, subordinate, or colleague.

However, people who come to an administrative counselor seldom come simply because of other people's problems. Deep-seated internal difficulties propel them unconsciously to seek help. But guilt or shame forces them to disguise the characteristics of their problems. As the counselor achieves rapport with the client, the inner world gradually emerges, and with it the gnawing, vexing disturbances heretofore hidden behind the mask of sophistication and maturity.

The Causes of Career Crisis

The executive who experiences an active career crisis tends to identify causes in the immediate administrative situation. He points the finger at specific objects and events, seemingly unaware of their relationship to his general career experience. If the reader recalls, the first thing Mark Whiting said when he came to the author for counseling was that the new president, Mr. Gray, should be on the psychologist's couch. He was convinced that the causes of his trouble were largely external to himself. This "externalizing" of one's anxiety is very common at the onset of a career crisis. Apparently the threat of a career crisis is too painful to be absorbed by the executive. It must be projected onto elements in the administrative scene.

The Freudian idea of a trauma, or wound, is widely accepted today, by both therapists and patients. The trauma concept pictures man as a machine which will continue to operate efficiently unless hit by a sharp blow. No account is given to the cumulative strain placed upon the machine through years of hard wear. In World War I, the term "shell shock" was attributed to brain damage caused by nearby explosions.

The trauma concept would suggest that the executive who received a lethal blow to his career potential was a fit subject for a career crisis. Using this concept, upwardly mobile men and women with basically positive orientation to their chances of success would be pictured in mid-life as potentially depressed when they took stock and realized that their youth had slipped away, their physical and mental capacities had been taxed to the limit in the struggle to get ahead, and that holding their own was becoming a firm value. However, some people in the middle years of life react less anxiously to their perceived limitations than others. Obviously, what is felt as trauma to some is not to others.

In this book we shall consider a different cause of a career crisis. We shall assume that the factors associated with mental disturbance are purely additive in their effects. The more negative experiences people have, the greater their mental health risk. Because no specific failures were directly associated with neuroses, the concept of a single "traumatic experience" must necessarily be questioned. Events in the life history of each executive seem to "pile up," increasing impairment, but there is not one event which by itself automatically spells career disaster for all who experience it.

In the counseling of executives, it appears that stressful events do not accumulate to a certain breaking point at which all executives are bound to collapse; the notion of the "straw that broke the camel's back" is not explanatory either of the incidence of career crisis. There is no "breaking point" in the number of factors beyond which there is a sudden marked increase in career difficulty. The data acquired from the counseling of men in career crisis seem to affirm this linear principle of the relationship of environmental stress factors to career difficulty. The concept of "the more, the unmerrier" seems to suggest that executives who show a sustained pattern of increasing administrative difficulty are more apt to be candidates for career crisis. They will feel their arrestment as more of a crisis than those who do not have this linear pattern. They have had several or many events in the past that have contributed to the felt crisis of today. These exents will be different for each executive, and they may be initially perceived as unique and separate. The difficulty of predicting who might undergo a felt crisis upon arrestment of upward mobility is related to the capacity of the individual to attach highly personal meanings to objects, events, and people. One man can acquire an idea of stress where another does not. All can continue to react to the idea of stress even when the stressful situation is no longer objectively real or present.

The mere anticipation of stress can be impairing for some. Some executives may react to the anticipation of arrestment in crisis-like terms, while others may require objective conditions of arrestment to be forcibly present. Administrative anxiety stems basically from anticipation of some future arrestment of achievements and mobility opportunity. The crisis may be the most extreme condition, possessing real clues to the impending arrestment. To say that a career crisis produces administrative anxiety is no more valid than to say that administrative anxiety produces a career crisis. Depending on the person, his history, and the interpretation of that history, any degree of administrative anxiety may be felt as a crisis in his career development. It is also proper to note that administrative anxiety may bring on the very career crisis which the anxiety is set to avoid.

What seems clear from the case studies of men in career crisis is the presence of a rather extended period of previous experiences associated with administrative difficulties that have not been successfully resolved and which tend to bring about the ordeal of a consciously-felt career crisis. The objective notions that one will never be better or more advanced than one is at present may actually serve to partially alleviate anxiety. Or they may cause the anxiety to become pervasive and spill over into allied activities.

The causes of a career crisis do not lie entirely in the childhood years. The executive career crisis is a product of a pattern of experiences acquired mostly in the adult years. Of course, there is no doubt that childhood experiences certainly lay the groundwork for the development of career disorder, but the life situation of the executive as he functions in the here and the now seems most clearly related to his present career possibilities. This means that the administrative counselor must analyze the present adult life situation for efficient screening and categorizing of psychological disturbances. To properly get at the underlying structure of the personality, he must understand the childhood experiences of his clients.

Shame and Guilt Anxiety

Counseling of executives in career crisis must take into account their feelings of *shame* and *guilt*. The dynamic basis of shame is the failure to live up to the requirements of administrative success. To the executive, success involves having little difficulty in performing the administrative role or in successfully overcoming great adversity. In either case, a career crisis represents failure and hence incurs shame.

Guilt is the feeling of having violated some codified norm or rule. The dynamic basis of guilt stems from the internalization of values of parents and other authority figures, the laws, regulations, and moral practices of society. Guilt is a response to highly codified and commonly accepted standards and practices. Feelings of guilt may be created by deviation from or violation of these standards and practices. These feelings are sustained by the censorship of the conscience, which has internalized these standards.

While guilt is the feeling of wrongdoing and is internal to the executive, shame is the feeling of being weak or inadequate and does not exist apart from the expressed scorn or disapproval of others. Guilt may be triggered by strictly internal cues about violations of highly codified standards and practices; shame may be triggered by external disapproval and scorn for deviation from uncodified standards and practices. There are really no legal or codified standards of success, especially executive success. Whatever standards exist are part and parcel of the requirements inherent in the executive role. Failure to live up to those requirements and expectations brings feelings of inadequacy and shame. The most important requirement is to maintain adequate functioning as an executive. Coming to a counselor for help is an acknowledgement of not functioning adequately. The counseling situation essentially evokes feelings of shame, and their understanding and removal may help to bring out more central underlying reasons for failure to perform the executive role adequately.

Shame is largely a surface symptom of the underlying anxiety of becoming separated from the executive role. As these feelings of shame are peeled off during the counseling relationship, the audiences which serve to heap scorn and disapproval begin to emerge. The major audience is the collective or commonly shared opinions of the executive group of which the executive is a member and in which he actively seeks maintenance of membership character. Two basic sets of expectations belong to this audience. One becomes a diffuse but discerned evaluation of whether the executive is pulling his weight in giving vital support to the goals of the corporation and their efficient achievement. The executive group has a capacity to sense who is really helping them perform the administrative functions of giving overall direction and character to the corporation. They tend to exchange eulogisms of the kind that reflect their esteem and satisfaction with each other. Feelings of pride are acquired from such positive affirmation. They also tend to evolve dyslogisms (opposite of eulogisms of praise and appreciation) of the kind that suggest dissatisfaction and disapproval. A dyslogism may be a minimization of what the executive has done, a tendency to negate his arguments, a pattern of interrupting his statements or not acknowledging their having been made, and so forth. Feelings of shame may be acquired from these negative regarding feelings of members of the executive group.

A second significant audience in the executive group is the authority figure or set constantly appraising and evaluating performance and fitness. The authority figure is concerned with whether to legitimatize or validate the role performance of the executive. He may give him the support of his superior authority while the remainder of the group members withhold affirmation. It is not uncommon for the executive to be viewed positively by the authority figure and negatively by the executive group as a whole. In such a case, he may feel pride mitigated by shame.

The Case of Stan**

In one particular case an executive, called Stan, produced a very restricted budget for his division that received immediate approval of the president and the chairman of the board. At the next meeting of the executive group, Stan was very coolly treated by members other than the president. Afterward, one colleague approached him with the suggestion that after this, he not embarrass them by failure to work out his budget concepts with them before submission to the boss.

In this case, authority-centered pride and group-centered shame provided a source of diffuse anxiety. Stan wanted to identify more with the group by conforming to their demands, but to do so might bring loss of support from the boss. The boss was very much a part of the executive group also. He had to maintain membership character in it due to the complexity of the administrative task in the large corporation. Separation from the group was as potentially threatening to him as the subordinate executive. Upon noticing severe disapproval of his legitimization of the subordinate executive, the president tried to reestablish his relationship by withdrawing some of his support from Stan. The latter conceived of this possibility too. Consequently, Stan felt an impending sense of danger from both boss and executive group. It is clear that Stan violated no highly codified, internalized law. His conscience did not tell him that he was a bad person. Rather, Stan had fallen short of a role-anchored expectation, which was felt as shame.

To illustrate guilt, we shall have to move to a standard or practice that is highly valued by all members of our society, and which is usually internalized by the child under the influence of parental control and guidance. One such codified norm is obedience to father and mother. In adult life, it is obedience to authority. Failure to obey may bring feelings of guilt. An executive who feels guilt has been mostly censored from within by his conscience.

The Case of George **

Guilt comes from a transgression that is not unique to the executive role, but may occur in any role or any institution in our society. The institution or the role merely serves as a vehicle for transgression and the inception of guilt reactions. In one case, a client, called George, became intensely unhappy with the behavior of the president of the corporation. In anger, George actively but secretly took upon himself the task of slicing the boss's throat by courting negative feelings in important members of the executive group. He and these several other group members began to gather data to support their doubts about the boss's competency, and eventually went to a small group outside board members. Convinced of the validity of their cause, they finally got a board rejection of the president. George was asked to assume the presidency and did so with apparent ease.

In a short while, he developed extreme feelings of inadequacy. George became indecisive, aloof, inaccessible, and hostile to the executive group. This hostility was followed by acts of extreme deference to and acceptance of the executive group. Movement back and forth between aggression and submission caused anxiety among the members of the group. They finally took overt action to have him ejected. In the career crisis that ensued, George evidenced considerable unconscious guilt for his acts of rebellion against the former president. It was apparent that this guilt had been repressed by means of justifying the incompetency of the president and the danger to the corporation. The repressed guilt, however, showed itself in the intense fear that the executive group would do to him what he had done to the predecessor. George became frozen in an unstable pattern of aggression-submission to the executive group.

The dictum obey your father and mother is a strong force making for prudent obedience to all authority figures. Those who have successfully internalized this moral directive are seldom without guilt anxiety when they take up arms against authority. Executives may feel guilt when they violate the essential authority of office, role, or superior figure. They may feel shame when they fail to live up to the work expectations of the executive group or the boss.

Guilt and shame may come from acts of disloyalty to the goals and needs of the corporation. The executive group is the chief interpreter of acts of disloyalty. If the executive fails to show the accepted sense of loyalty to the corporation, he may become the brunt of scorn and disapproval. He may merely be showing acts of loyalty that are not commonly accepted by other members of the executive group. In such a case, shame may be felt because of his deviation. Guilt may not enter in if his conscience gives him support for his intense but unacceptable loyalty to the corporation.

Guilt may ensue if he violates his conscience. The directive of loyalty is deep-seated in the personality of most members of our society. It goes back to loyalty to mother and family, who are perceived and felt by the child to be synonymous. It is the mother's home, not the father's, owing to the frequent absence of the latter and omnipresence of the former. Loyalty to the virtue and values of the mother carries over to provide generalized loyalty to the family, school, community, and nation. It has been shown in research dealing with combat crews in World War II that those most capable of sacrificing life for country were those who had stable and secure attachments to mother and family. The studies of business executives show that when this attachment is not developed, or when it is broken with aggression and hostility, the executive has difficulty identifying with the goals and achievement of the corporation. To be against the corporation is a violation of the emotional directive inhering in the conscience of the typical executive.

In clinical practice, it is not infrequent to find executives who have accepted the advantages and satisfactions of upward mobility and success without the positive emotional attachments to the corporation. They invariably reveal a repressed pattern of guilt based upon their drive for self-centered rewards and satisfactions. A career crisis may ensue because of the capacity of other executives at the top to sense self-centered ambitions and basic corporation indifference and disloyalty. The negative cues provided by the executive group may set off a chain of guilt reactions in the executive that may be every bit as debilitating as those set off by disloyalty to authority. The boss and the corporation are symbolic heirs to the parent and family figures. Violation of their values, directives, and expectations may bring guilt. The guilt may become repressed, giving rise to symptoms of anxiety to allay problems of authority and organization achievement.

In a career crisis, symbolic representations of authority and organization are fused with notions of self. Guilt and shame involve feelings of selfhood. The child's notions of self gradually emerge from the matrix of parental and family relationships. Acts of guilt and shame may lead to violation of notions of self. As in the case of the executive, Stan, who attempted to re-identify with the executive group, the individual may become a submissive conformist in order to allay his anxiety of separation. In so doing he may not like what he sees in himself. His notions of being an autonomous person who can stand on his own feet may press against his picture of a practicing sycophant. Wanting to submit to allay anxiety of separativeness, he may incur the anxiety of lost self-respect. Guilt and shame may be an inner recoil to one's own violation of selfhood. Doubt of oneself is intermeshed with acts of loyalty and disloyalty to authority and organization.

The executive group tends to be the chief interpreter of the acts of loyalty and disloyalty to authority and organization that bring feelings of shame within the executive. The individual himself (his internal directives of conscience) tends to be the chief interpreter of acts of loyalty and disloyalty that bring feelings of guilt. Pure cases of guilt and shame are rare. The executive usually experiences fused mixtures of the two. In this fusion—violation of primitive taboos originating in childhood, and violation of role-anchored taboos emerging from the unique properties of the administrative group—may be found the essential characteristics of the career crisis. Primitive or contrived notions of authority, organization, and self must be separated and analyzed to get at the dynamic basis of the administrative anxiety.

Executive Isolation

Feelings of guilt and shame involve feelings of isolation. The executive desires to be attached to the central administrative processes of the firm. Charged with the administrative responsibility, the executive group exerts enormous power over the individual who aspires to become and remain a member executive. Guilt represents inner directives that make him feel isolated from this important group. Shame represents external directives that make the executive feel isolated. The absence of feelings of shame implies the acceptance of the validity of the executive group's distinct ways of organizing its activities. Such norms and standards are highly specific to the group and may be different from one firm to another. The absence of feelings of guilt implies the acceptance of the validity of the basic notions of authority and organization that are general to the society of which the firm is a part. A basic quality of the individual is his capacity to feel guilt and shame. Without such capacity, it is difficult to conceive of any lasting element of authority and organization in society.

The big corporation requires a high degree of emotional investment and commitment. Men at the top show a marked capacity to avoid feelings of guilt and shame. Such a capacity is derived from experience in pre-adult institutions and is maintained and developed by continuous exposure to the requirements of authority and organization within the business firm. The avoidance of guilt and shame most often occurs in the productive expression of the unique powers of the self. The individual learns how and when to conform and to make changes that result in validation of role and self. This is the constructive response to guilt and shame. The self becomes more fully realized.

Self-damage, rather than self-realization, may result from acute feelings of guilt and shame and the incapacity to productively discharge them. The individual may partially though inadequately allay anxiety by developing either overly hostile or dependent patterns of behavior. Hostility is more easily detected and more morally devalued. Consequently, hostility is less often resorted to, especially by those who move successfully to the top. This means that the aggressive type is less common. The major pattern is conformity and deference.

In a career crisis, a few executives have the overwhelming urge to throw themselves upon the mercies of the executive group. This is essentially a neurotic substitute for constructive resolution of the essential anxiety. It is unproductive because, rather than allaying anxiety, it really breeds more anxiety, owing to the damage to positive notions of self and the arrestment of the powers of self-realization. The executive in a career crisis may be apt to have used the deference pattern somewhat productively in previous states of anxiety. He may overreact to the present danger of separation from the executive group because he has a large residue of anxiety carried over from previous attempts at deference and submissiveness. In some cases, only a few weak notions of self remain, so thoroughly has the identity of the executive been damaged. This man may then become alienated from his real self, separated emotionally from the executive group and from the central administrative activities of the firm. Executive isolation is typically multifaceted and pervasive and may extend beyond the confines of the executive role to include other life areas.

The Case of Paul **

Executive crises may be vast and complex in their impact upon society, but they revolve around problems of authority, goals, needs of the organization, and self-notions of the executive. Several years ago an executive, whom we shall call Paul, came to the author with a problem that later erupted into a national scandal. Since there were many executives from numerous corporations involved in the electrical manufacturing price collusion conspiracy, this particular case may be partially described. Paul's concern was that he had been given cues to the effect that he should join in this collusion as a basis of job tenure and promotion. Yet these messages were only indirect and could not be easily substantiated. The thought of engaging in this affair was not permissible to his concept of the kind of a person he was and wanted to become. Paul asked for professional help in evolving an extrication strategy that would enhance his notions of self without violating his superior's cues and without grossly jeopardizing his chances for advancement.

However, it was a very difficult strategy to devise because his superior could easily ascertain whether prices in his division were being rigged or not. If they were not, Paul would be held responsible. Because he had not the formal authority, nor the conscience, the case was tricky. The client grew despondent and depressed, fighting alternating fits of aggression and submission, only to face another attempt at adjustment. One day, in a state of anxiety, he sought to confront his superior and determine just exactly what was expected. At this point Paul was told by his superior, "Whatever you do, you do on your own, but please get it done."

Against professional counsel and his conscience, he went to a meeting of representatives of other firms and joined in price rigging. Several days later, he returned for guidance in a state of acute anxiety. Paul was utterly disturbed by the thought that he would get caught and no one would back him up. It became evident that his notions of self were now involved mostly in the fear of getting caught and not in the ethical problem. This being the case, a strategy was devised to minimize the chances of being caught and punished. From then on, he represented the corporation's welfare in these transactions effectively and received the approval of the authority system by increased responsibility. His promotion did not remove him from the collusive activities, but rather made him responsible for more of these types of transactions. However, Paul's anxiety level gradually lowered. He came eventually to believe that the corporation required this kind of effort and that he should encourage subordinates to aid the effort, whenever and wherever justified.

Paul's career crisis, however, was just beginning. Some time later, he and several dozen other executives from the electrical manufacturing industry were found guilty in a Philadelphia court of law and fined, and in some cases sentenced. Paul was sentenced and dismissed from his corporation, which absolved itself of any responsibility for his activities. Judge Ganey remarked, "I am convinced that in the great number of these defendant's cases, they were torn between conscience and an approved corporate policy, with the rewarding objective of promotion, comfortable security and large salaries—in short, the organization or the company man, the conformist, who goes along with his superiors and finds balm for his conscience in additional comforts and the security of his place in the corporate setup."

In these few words, Judge Ganey gave an apt description of anxiety and how it is sometimes dealt with. The expectations of the boss, the requirements of the corporation in an oligopolistic industry, and the conscience of the individual were hung together in a conflicting pattern of psychic tension. Something had to give. Notions of a moral person became partially blurred and gave way to the powerful notions of a successful, dutiful, loyal executive. As the executive stood to hear sentence, he was flooded with his now active notions of what kind of a person he once wanted to become. Shame and guilt drove him into a deep state of withdrawal. His premature death may be largely accounted for by his lost sense of identity and self-worth.

Cue Anxiety

In a career crisis, the question concerning the executive role is always related to the client's perceived position in the corporation in general and the executive group in particular. Thus a senior vice-president of a large chemical company may define his job much differently than a general manager of a division in an automobile company. Likewise, a staff advisor to the president in charge of corporate planning may tend to see different meanings in his job than a line vice-president in charge of marketing. Also, a career crisis centered around the problem of being fired or retired may call for different meanings than a career crisis centered around thwarted aspirations for the presidency.

An administrative counselor has no particular tricks that will help to dissolve the crisis. The typical tools associated with clinical psychology and psychiatry are useless if the client cannot perform more productively in the managerial role. In the final analysis, the administrative counselor must be able to help the executive formulate a more productive solution of the administrative job than what he brought to the task originally. Some executives may have unproductive notions of authority that block either their handling of their own authority or their relating properly to authority figures. Other executives may have notions of organization that prohibit adaptive and productive responses. Still others have notions of self, inflated or deflated beyond realistic proportions, that restrict their managerial effectiveness. Whatever these notions are, they must be systematically examined in the light of what is generally known about the managerial task.

The corporation is not a hospital. For this reason therapy cannot directly involve enlisting the support of other people in the corporation to dissolve the executive's anxieties. An executive's career crisis can be resolved largely by helping him to become a better administrator. Becoming a better administrator necessarily involves insight into what kinds of tools are being used or abused. One tool is the utilization of cues, rather than spoken words, to show direction, intention, support, indifference, disapproval, and scorn. In the executive group much of what is expected is not directly stated.

The use of cues is based upon the reluctance to confront a colleague directly because of the potential damage to self-esteem. At the executive level, notions of self are usually quite strong, and the satisfaction of their maintenance prohibits aggressive confrontation of another person. There is also the growing practice to minimize overt authority and emphasize solidarity and cohesion as ways to achieve compliance. This is a general pattern in our society and a highly prevalent one in the big corporation where the executive group, of which the president is a member, is the chief unifying agency between the corporation as a whole and the subdivisions. Combat, then, is a more subtle affair. One way to remove undesirable people from the central administrative process of the firm is to disenfranchise them.

The Case of Bill **

One executive, called Bill, faced the possibility of being disenfranchised by the executive committee. This meant that he would not be allowed an opportunity to effect the outcome of certain crucial matters. This would not have constituted a danger had it not been that he was the manager of a high priority division. If Bill could not help determine the direction and character of the total corporation, he could not substantially control this major division. He saw his future at stake. Yet, no one really told him that he was disenfranchised. Bill gradually perceived that decisions were being made that were more responsive to other division heads' requirements and expectations. At first, he cautiously checked to see if his suspicions were correct. They were.

In counseling, it became apparent that Bill had been here before, so to speak. He recalled that at least twice before he had been gradually excluded from the decision-making apparatus at lower managerial levels. One time Bill panicked and concentrated his energy on leaving the corporation and finding employment elsewhere. Another time he rode out the crisis by a process of associating with those who could restore his prestige and influence. On these two previous occasions, Bill was younger and had time to start over again or to slowly disarm the skeptics. Now Bill was fifty-two and committed to the corporation. He could not take five or ten years to recover lost prestige because he was in a high priority division, and men do not last long if they cannot help control the affairs of the corporation in general. He had to act fast, but how? What could Bill do that would be responsive to the rapidly developing situation? He knew that in his corporation a man could be in one day and out the next. His was a swift, emerging corporate world in which men could be quickly made and broken. Besides, he was so near to being the next corporation president that he could not give up. The tailspin, at first, was only a faint spiral whose turns grew more acute with the growing evidence of disenfranchisement.

No doubt it was the authority system that made the decisions, but who actually started the cycle? Bill had a powerful position in the organization as the marketing vice-president, but how could this help him now? What did he really want to do to alleviate the situation? What kind of constraints would his notion of the kind of person he was exert at this time?

In his career crisis, the immediate danger was in some way related to his role in the corporation and the impressions and expectations of the authority set, including the president. The danger was perceived as threatening to his notions of the kind of person he was and wished to become. He felt the danger, felt somewhat helpless, and faintly recalled having been in this box before. He turned to a friend, who encouraged him to get administrative counsel.

Anxiety is almost always associated with the inner danger of unacceptable thoughts, feelings, wishes, or drives which elicit the expectations of some kind of harm, loss, disapproval, or punishment. Harm to self, loss of status and prestige, loss of useful employment of his resources, peer disapproval, and corporate disenfranchisement in the form of demotion, shelving, or early forced retirement were perceived as possible.

It was apparent that the prevalent use of cues should force the executive to utilize cues to alleviate his condition. But Bill did not see it this way. He brought his presumed disenfranchisement out into the open, much to the embarrassment of the other members of the executive group. The reaction was lethal. It was much as though this executive group believed that return thrusts should be based upon the manner in which the original offensive action was delivered. The executive group further did not believe such things should be brought up in a group atmosphere. They vigorously denied Bill's accusations and harshly admonished him for harboring ill thoughts about them. Some had made up their minds that because of his indiscretion, he was obviously not suitable for the performance of the executive role. In private, one suggested to Bill that he might want to take an extended vacation. He had obviously overworked himself. The president thought of this solution also. This suggestion, although coming from independent sources, was interpreted as evidence of the ganging up on him that produced his disenfranchisement. Bill had direct confirmation now and resolved that the last thing he was going to do was to leave the scene and have his job completely emasculated.

A career crisis may be aggravated by petite paranoia, a response quite common among disturbed executives who cannot hold up under the anxiety of the cue system. For Bill, therapy constituted breaking through this wall of paranoiac isolation and gaining realistic estimates of the intent of the authority set, the potential or silent opportunities to show usefulness to the corporate goals, and restoration of lost self-confidence.

Career Defense

The career crisis invariably marks the first step in the process leading to neuroses. The executive becomes inhibited and restrained in his capacity to be aware of reality. Turning away from reality, failing to allow it to register meaningfully is a decisive step toward distortion or inhibition of the creative processes. The individual's choices of behavior are diminished by the degree to which reality is distorted. Awareness of externalities becomes transferred to the drives to restore lost attachments. This restoration becomes the overriding value. Lost is the notion that the reality of corporation life prohibits action outside the context of the administrative role. Stan failed to understand the relative uselessness of sentiment. It is not possible to go to the aggressor and plead for forgiveness. However, sentiment often caused Stan to appraise unrealistically the executive role.

Separation from the executive group may be stemmed by understanding what is essentially valued by the group. The crucial value is maintained of their established patterns, and practices, their essential integrity of function. This is highly related to corporate goals and the authority set. Attachment can only be made within the confines of the executive group and the role perceived as valid for the executive. Therapy constitutes splitting of the ego, whereby the awareness-of-reality part is discovered by the client and used in cooperation with the objectivity of the counselor. Unless there is a realistic awareness, therapy can not be achieved. However, in administrative anxiety, realistic awareness is still highly present in contrast to cases of acute neuroses. The reality that is adequately perceived and the capacity to perceive reality are enlisted in defense of the distorted perceptions of the career crisis.

When the executive feels threatened by the impending danger of separation from the central administrative processes, attention narrows and he may confine his interest to the immediate situation. This is called "tunnel vision" and is represented by repression of thoughts unacceptable to the self. The results is a highly simplified version of what has happened. The executive seems to maintain this simplified version as though it were a source of security. Such tendency shows up in impatience with the investigating aspects of the preliminary diagnostic interviews, an urgent demand for prompt confirmation by the counselor, and an incessant requesting for easy solutions. A simplified version calls out for a comprehensive solution—a solution that will work now and forever. This tendency serves to place a high expectation upon the counselor, which if not immediately fulfilled will develop disappointment.

Positive notions of self are highly prized by the executive, particularly those notions of what kind of an executive he is and how well others think of him. A career crisis essentially means that the notions of self anchored in the executive role are threatened. When this signal of danger to self is felt, defenses may be brought into play that have as their main purpose maintaining the integrity of the self. A common mechanism of defending notions of self is aggression. Attacking the aggressor conflicts with the reality of the executive role. This must not be done. Rather, utilizing the energies of anger by sublimating them in the form of constructive administrative activity must be encouraged.

Defense of the self may be performed by projecting hostility and anxiety into others. The executive may defend himself against attack by believing that others are under attack as well. His picture of what has happened may be partially softened by picturing others as facing a similar threat. Or he may defend himself by incorporating the aggressor. The executive may unconsciously attempt to allay anxiety by taking on the attributes of the threatening figure. He may identify with the values and beliefs of the executive group or authority figure or a significant other. The strength and power of the threatening object becomes the basis of his strength and power.

Just as he may attempt to defend self, he may attempt to enhance self as a basis of maintaining positive notions of self. He may overly strengthen his self-notions to a point of idealization. He may come to feel highly inflated and superior. Such idealization of self may cause disastrous consequences. One very common result is to engage in a withdrawal pattern. Believing himself superior and too good for the kind of treatment he is receiving, he may simply discount the danger. Instead of releasing energy in a constructive form, he may withdraw it. The signs may be indifference, aloofness, and condescension. All of these forms of withdrawal send out lethal cues that are negatively evaluated by members of the executive group. Condescension not only causes others to react even more aggressively, but brings a grossly underestimated definition to events in the situation that unfolds during the career crisis.

In either self-defensive or self-enhancing mechanisms, the symbolic object may be the authority figure or set, or the corporate goals and traditions, or both. In some self-enhancing defenses, notions of self may become idealized at the diminution of the value of the corporate goals and traditions. The corporation symbolizes what the executive feels is inferior to his beliefs. Competition, profits, good public relations, and cost-mindedness may become devalued. In their place may be valued such activities as those that are characterized by the career crisis.

The Case of Harry **

Harry consistently failed to run his division in a profitable way. His return on capital invested in his division by the corporation was far too low to be considered satisfactory. His career crisis was largely caused by this continued pattern. He wanted to be more efficient, but could not. His crisis became acutely aggravated by his direct insistence that profitability was not really everything. He prided himself on his permissive style of administration. He felt the necessity to assert this style when it was presumably under attack. He set up a program to encourage the development of a more cooperative type of manager within his division. The response from on top was firm and negative. In the attempt to avoid this threat to self, Harry lashed out at the values of the corporation. He pled for help by his request for a more considerate, cooperative form of enterprise. He vigorously asserted those values which were covertly aimed at giving him the emotional support he desperately wanted. He placed himself in the position of moral arbiter and statesman. All others who were "profit oriented" felt the sting of his aggressiveness. His self-enhancement met with severe repercussions.

A defence of self may elicit a self-effacement pattern. Here the executive identifies with his negative notions of self. He turns away from any notion that he is equal to the task. Feelings of superiority and eventual triumph are repressed. He grows smaller and smaller in his own eyes, invites abuse, belittlement and further degradation. The appeal of going to pieces and submitting to the actions of the aggressor becomes inviting. It becomes tempting for him to give credence to even the most sinister implication of danger to his career. His career is all over; he invites the worst of all possibilities, yes, even accepts them.

Lost Reality

In both defensive enhancing and effacing solutions, the turning away from reality is common. A career crisis is a threat to self and, as such, can be realistically confronted by only the most courageous. The result for many is the feeling of being "bad" or "weak." Guilt and shame may be inextricably fused to make feelings of isolation greater than the actual degree of possibility of separation from the central tasks of the executive group.

Feelings of guilt and shame are difficult to communicate. They are repressed, rather than released, because of their potential threat to positive notions of self. The counselor's willingness to understand, his faith in the client's potentialities, his objectivity and firmness in not becoming absorbed into the client's incipient neuroses, his unflagging concern for reality, all become the vital balance and basis of therapy.

It is also crucial to realize that the executive group does not offer a basis of identification because it is simply a group. The attractiveness of the group transcends the peculiar organization of it, or even the characteristics of its membership. The executive group is a magnet because of its essential concern with the central administrative tasks of the corporation. The executive may identify with the authority system and the superior figure who represents that system, or he may identify with the goals and purposes of the corporation. In either case, the executive group serves as the means whereby this identification is made practical. The case of John may serve to illustrate. Remember that the motives to associate with the goals and values of the corporation may be to allay separation anxiety. The specific source of the anxiety may be in the executive's relationship to the authority set or the boss himself.

The Case of John **

In this man's case, the boss, and subsequently the executive group, placed formidable barriers to his maintaining proper degrees of power and influence with subordinates in the organization. Subsequently, John acquired an intense concern for the corporation, its future and welfare. His interviews revealed the presence of a secondary identification pattern (with corporation) to remove the original source of anxiety.

John's attempt to resolve his anxiety placed him in a triangle of conflicting emotions. He saw his boss and the authority set as definitely threatening, bringing on a crisis involving his notions of self. A crisis of self is commonly precipitated by the aggressive or dominating action of another person or object in the subject's immediate environment. Further, the individual feels no available inner resources for dealing with the crisis as it is represented. Theoretically, John had many alternatives. One was that he could have identified with the aggressive object, the boss in specific, or the authority set of the executive group. But this alternative was not open to him. John had a previous history of dealing with authority problems by associating and identifying with the organization with which the authority figure was primarily concerned. In his childhood, when his father threatened him with punishment, John was seen later to be striving hard in the routine work patterns of the home. Specifically, he would appear to the father as more conscious of the needs of the family, showing more responsibility than might be expected of a child of his age and size. He would aggressively enter into social activities and thus find subsequent relief from the father's wrath. In school, and later in the work system, he tended to avoid the wrath of the teacher or boss by his concern for the goals and activities of the situation. Although John was partly conscious of having used this pattern of reaction, he was not conscious of how much he had relied upon it in the past.

Because of his inherent capacity to work and his desire to receive a high payoff, he was always interested in knowing the goals and achieving their implementation. This association with the organization, coupled with strong identification growing out of occasional conflicts with authority figures, provided John with an enduring reputation as a corporation man. Inwardly, however, he used his aggressive achievement as a strategic device to acquire authority. His continuing hope was to become president some day.

Authority to him was the measure of man. The men above were viewed as important, wise, extra-capable people. In the performance of his junior executive roles, he enjoyed the thrill of commanding and receiving obedience, and felt anger when his commands were not eagerly obeyed. With subordinates he learned to pitch his commands within the framework of the objective necessities of the organization. This administrative style paid great dividends, except when he came into conflict with superiors who deemed themselves more capable than he of interpreting the objective necessities of the corporation. His strong desire to be one of them was countered inwardly by a suspicion and distrust of them. Thus he occasionally would be distrusted by them and would have his effectiveness diminished thereby. Not knowing how to directly confront the authority figure to exchange information and achieve adequate clarification, he resorted to a positive onslaught upon the corporate goals and needs. Always in the past this administrative style had worked, although he did not know why he pursued this pattern of identification. Identification means that the subject behaves in a way that is subjectively like that of the object. The corporation stood for certain things at each level of his career rise, and these values became completely, rigidly adhered to.

John's arrestment of increasing authority and power occurred because significant members of the authority set persuaded the boss that great changes had to be made in order to take advantage of certain markets and supplier opportunities. These individuals convinced the boss that certain economy measures coming from John's department accounted for their present market difficulties. The president decided that perhaps new corporate designs must be developed and that John might not be effective in their devising and implementation. These decisions came to John through the medium of interpersonal communication with several colleagues.

The signals of possible rejection from the central administrative process aroused anxiety that automatically triggered an enlarged and aggressive pattern of identification with the established goals and values of the corporation. At a time when these were under indictment, John nevertheless affirmed them totally and rigidly. The result was to set John on an unalterable collision course. The boss formally relieved him of all marketing duties and placed him in a job as manager of special operations. Literally, he was given problems that never needed to be solved. The actual separation from central administrative responsibility was too much. He broke down completely under the strain and was given competent medical treatment. When he was sufficiently recovered, he was provided with administrative counseling.

Under conditions of stress and strain, John's inflated notions of the importance of authority gave rise to instrumental use of the corporation's goal and values. By the successful implementation of this administrative style, John was able to realistically see himself as being the boss someday. His instrumental use of corporate goals which had worked on previous occasions, at the end actually caused his formal removal from office and precipitated an emotional collapse. John's case illustrates the problem of restriction of reality awareness under conditions of acute anxiety. He could not see that he was on a collision course, even though there was considerable objective evidence to predict his impending disaster.

In conclusion, notions of self are related to notions of authority and organization. The vehicle for the crystallization of notions of self, authority, and organization is the executive group. Its fascination and power lies in its responsibility to administer the overall goals and purposes of the organization. The executive measures success by how intimately he is involved in the central administrative processes of the firm. Separation from the executive group amounts to separation from these central tasks. The danger of separation signals threats to self. A career crisis becomes a crisis of self.

5

WHY EXECUTIVES REBEL OR CONFORM

The business executive is mastered by a single force. It is something deep inside of him that is a product of his childhood experiences. It is the drive to achieve. To *achieve* means to perform increasingly challenging tasks. Early in his career he sees that the more challenging jobs are arranged hierarchically upward. The corporate ladder allows him to set his sights upward, using each round to show proficiency for a higher round. At any given level he experiences impatience. He dare not enjoy the assignment too much or relax too much. He must prepare to depart shortly after he arrives at any point in his emerging career.

The business executive does not enjoy the plateaus between achievements. He is never satisfied with himself, his successes and opportunities; for each new success he posts higher goals for himself. The achievement drive increases geometrically to eventually become insatiable. For this reason he can never relax and enjoy internal rest.

Men who arrive at the top have reputations. They are known for having done things differently. Achievement, in order to be meaningful to them, means making things happen their way. Their efforts must largely ensue from their choices if they are to count. This eminently qualifies such men to be innovators or change agents. But to be an innovator the potential executive must have more than a high need to achieve. Mark Whiting and Will Fowler had high needs to accomplish challenging assignments. Both were overwhelmed by events and forces not of their own choosing. In spite of terrific punishment, neither has given up. Their powerful drive to get things done is being channeled effectively because they understand better the kinds of forces that bombard members who penetrate the business world. These forces are not unique. Rather, some executives have a built-in capacity to handle these pressures better than others. The pressures of corporate existence are basically three. The first set of pressures come from superiors who have the power to give and withhold rewards of all kinds. Then, there are the pressures that come from the goals and objectives of the organization as felt in the executive's particular job. Lastly, there are the pressures that come from within the executive himself. These pressures come from his definition of who he is and what he wants to become. These three sets of pressures are always present in varying degrees, even before a career crisis strikes. But when it strikes, they become superactive, and if mastery is delayed, they will eventually clog the whole mind, driving out other pressures or giving them a secondary prominence. What emerges from an extended career crisis is a triangle of pressures interlocked in a way that suggests wholeness. This is the corporate triangle.

How the Corporate Triangle Aids Mobility

Life in the corporate triangle is a convenient way to express the activity of the mind caught up with the pressures of a career crisis. The mental life of this executive pivots on a triad of pressures.

An executive in a career crisis tends to focus on problems of authority and goal achievement activities of the corporation. These factors are, in turn, evaluated in terms of the kind of person the executive believes he is and would like to become. His notions of self are intermingled with his notions of what the president or chairman of the board or some superior expects of him and what the corporate goals actually require of him. Few career crises may be understood without ascertaining these notions of authority, organization, and self. The executive in a career crisis comes prepared to focus decisively upon these few notions and charge them with both highly causal and productive values.

The corporate triangle becomes activated abnormally during

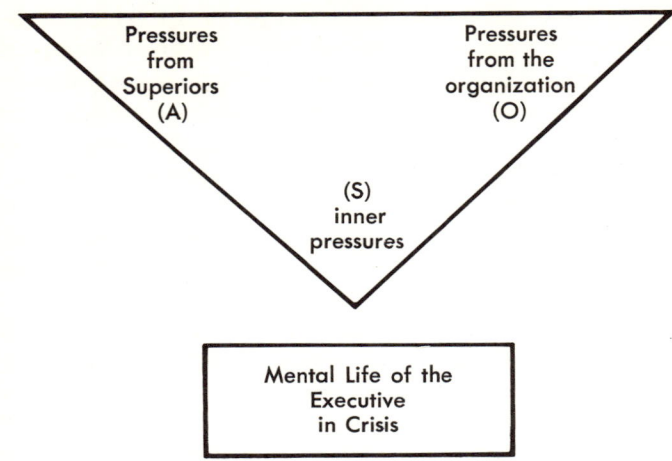

a career crisis. It is not created at this time. The corporate triangle exists in all executives to some degree, regardless of their career difficulties. It grows out of a need to make sense of their highly complex environments. This process of making sense is initially a simplifying exercise. From a myriad of forces and situations, only a few emerge upon which they base their career patterns.

In the mind of the big business executive, the authority system and its crucial members are identified apart from other features of the corporate environment. The reason the executive learns to single out the authority group is because effective performance does not identify itself. Performance is judged as effective by someone who is in a position to know and has the necessary resources to evaluate and approve. The executive looks to authority figures for their approval of his achievements. Evaluation and legitimatization emanate from authority figures. To win their blessings, the executive must know how to relate to them, to learn from them, and, by access to them, gain the necessary resources to fulfill the achievement drive. In this way the achievement drive becomes oriented toward the values and expectations of the authority system. The mobile executive has the necessary facilities to relate properly to the authority system. He believes that authority figures are necessary and useful, but, at the same time, distrusts them enough to rely upon his own resources.

While his achievement drive compels him to do things his way, his notions of authority compel him to receive his superior's blessing. He resolves this conflict by working hard to make his boss look good and then engineering support for his unique orientations and views. A superior and subordinate who work in close harmony in this way will together provide a package of skills and achievements that are highly prized by the corporation. The impact upon the organization of two such men who together are crucially effective is far greater than any two individuals working less coordinately; for this reason, superiors and subordinates who are crucial to each other's effectiveness tend to move up together. Mobility is based upon mutual achievement. The capacity to enhance the effectiveness of another is a basic prerequisite of garnering trust. Few men get to the top of the big business corporation who are not trusted by someone already there. Achievement plus trust spells high upward mobility.

The mobile executive singles out another part of the corporate environment. This is the corporation's goals, policies, and values as they are found in each of his positions in his emerging career; to these factors he lends his achievement drive. Achievement becomes effective when executing these requirements and demands. In any position, conflict may develop between what the corporation expects of him and what he wants to do. He must live up to the norms and expectations that follow from the objectives and policies of the corporation. His innovative thrust is given form and direction within boundaries established by the corporation's goals and policies that are found in his station.

As he gains effectiveness and support, he may be asked to help define the objectives and policies under which he and others must achieve. Now his innovative potential is released in terms which more fully realize his drive to make things happen his way. As he nears the top of the corporate ladder, he is given still wider freedom to release his need to achieve. At the top, he experiences the thrill of attempting to change the direction and character of the corporate enterprise. What makes life at the top exciting is the feeling of mastery and sense of identity that the opportunities afford. His notions of self become affirmed by success.

The rocky road to the top is a journey into self-insight and development. Executing within the demands and expectations of the authority set and corporate objectives and policies calls for strong internal controls. An individual with a high need to achieve, to get things done his way, needs these internal controls that keep a check on impulsive performance. In the course of his career, these internal controls are usually strengthened adequately to fulfill the achievement drive. When they are not sufficiently strengthened, difficulty will eventually ensue.

The cases of Mark Whiting and Will Fowler are instructive at this point. Both executives had difficulty gearing their high achievement drive to the norms and expectations of authority figures. When they finally acquired the necessary discipline, they moved ahead rapidly. At the near top, these internal controls on their achievement drive became weakened. They moved disastrously against the powers to be and lost forever the presidency. We shall present the cases of Olaf Johnson and Oscar Hanson to illustrate the lack of internal controls that prohibits proper adjustment to the demands of organizational life. The case of Sam Cory will illustrate the lack of both authority and organization oriented internal controls.

When any one of these three anchorages becomes too set or too weak, the other two are adversely affected. In a way, the executive loses his balance. He leans too much toward one angle of the triangle. He may become authority-centered, organization-centered, or self-centered. The unbalanced executive allows his achievement drive to be too much or too little directed by any one component of this triangle. Career difficulty may develop eventually. The probability of career arrestment is high but not sufficient to guarantee it. The unbalancing of the corporate triangle is a necessary but not a sufficient cause of career arrestment. The necessary causes inhere in the situation. Perhaps if another person had been president, or if another person besides Mr. Gray had succeeded to the presidency, Mark Whiting would be more alive career-wise than he is today.

We shall present the cases of Neal Powers and Norman Wells to illustrate how a career crisis may not restore the balanced posture of the executive. Under the right circumstances, an unbalanced executive may actually be promoted to the top position. Also, Neal Powers and Norman Wells had sufficient internal controls to disguise their distorted orientations. Mark Whiting apparently did not. His distrust of authority became too apparent, whereas Neal Powers and Norman Wells were able to hide their neurotic tendencies by latching onto favorable situational circumstances. Their neuroses actually exploited an emerging situation. More typically, however, an unbalanced orientation will prevent mobility to the top. The unbalancing of the corporate triangle and the presence of individuals who may react negatively to the distortions spell career arrestment in a vast majority of cases.

But career arrestment may not throw every executive into a state of acute anxiety. Some executives gradually adjust to stopping at levels lower than the presidency. The cases in this book represent men who were not able to make this adjustment smoothly. In fact, their career arrestment greatly affected their whole style of life.

From these case histories it will become apparent that the achievement drive is frustrated without proper notions of authority and organization. But the mobile executive has a third anchorage upon which he builds his career pattern. He simplifies his environment by supplying specific notions of who he is and what he wants to do and become. The executive's notions of self constantly exert pressure upon him. He must achieve in terms of these inner expectations before performance becomes achievement to him; from his specific achievements he derives his sense of identity. Men at the top know who they are and what they want to do. They typically have strong, clear images of self. The Mark Whitings and Will Fowlers were the exceptions to this fact until they mastered their career crises.

At any point along this path to the top, the executive's notions of self may get out of line with the requirements of authority and organization. Sam Cory acquired an inflated and idealized notion of self that prohibited serving authorities and corporate objectives effectively. Impoverished notions of self may prohibit innovative behavior too. The individual may become merely an extension of a boss who uses him as a yes man. Just as there are few Sams at the top, so are there few with weak, impoverished notions of self.

The executive learns to master his complex environment by the development of three orientations, each of which is related to the other two. He must achieve within the boundaries set forth by the expectations and demands of the authority, organization, and self systems. In turn, he must learn to levy expectations and demands upon the corporate triangle. Without the latter, achievement does not occur. If he does not fulfill the expectations of the former, the latter will not be possible. Achievement is made possible by living up to and changing these systems of expectations and demands of his corporate environment.

The Case of Hawley Simpson *

We shall attempt to reconstruct some of the more stress-producing administrative patterns. The authority-centered pattern represents an executive whose career crisis seems anchored around the relationship between notions of self and the wider authority system of which his self is a part. In Diagram ACA(1) the relative distances of these lines show this pattern of orientation.

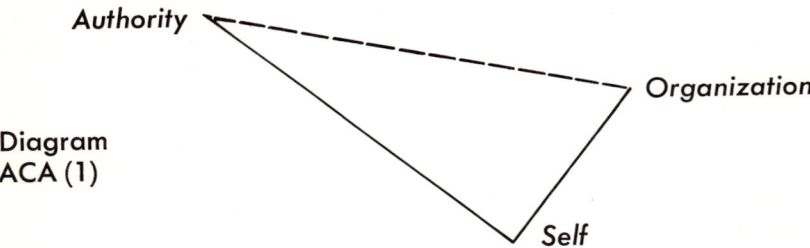

Diagram ACA (1)

The executive feels moderately close to the goals, policies, and procedures of the corporation (S-O) as well as those that are represented in his particular managerial situation. His drive to get things done has been productively applied in the services of these organizational forces and requirements. However, notice the greater distance of the self from his authority set. This represents a feeling of being distant from his superiors. The boss is felt to be threatening and is also perceived as emotionally distant from the organization. He feels that he is better attuned to the needs of the corporation than his bosses.

Generally, in such a pattern it is found that the executive has always been unconsciously afraid of authority. In childhood he may have viewed parents and parental surrogates with highly negative regarding tendencies for their power and freedom. He may have reacted acutely to the use of their power differentials against him in punishment and corrective efforts. But because hatred of parents is an act against the conscience, the boy may have repressed his negative feelings, and thus may have created a strong desire to be like one of them in his adult life. Lurking behind this positive identification may be the hostility that was never allowed to work itself out. Always he has some feelings of restriction in the presence of superiors. Occasionally, these anxieties break out.

The case of Hawley Simpson is especially relevant. He had this inner hostility overlaid by close feelings of identification with authority figures. When Hawley Simpson failed them or they turned irrationally against him, he overreacted as though they were so powerful that he was incapable of handling them. In his developing career, his ambivalence was allayed by directly making stronger identification with the goals, policies, rules, and regulations of the corporation. He learned to allay his authority-centered anxieties by developing an administrative style that was sensitive to realistic and practical goal-setting and an efficient organization to achieve such goals. He became known as a high achiever. His superiors noted that in his upper-middle management positions he had great organizing ability. He exuded corporate loyalty and took over assignments courageously and enthusiastically.

Hawley Simpson became a member of the executive group at the age of forty. He dug into the job of helping set long-range strategy by acceptance of corporate planning responsibility. Although for the most part the executive group worked closely together on proposing and revising strategical goals, Hawley Simpson was often deferred to in matters of reorganization necessary to implement these corporate strategies. Although his behavior showed great corporate loyalty, actually he felt only moderately close to the corporation and to the goals he helped to achieve. He felt that emotional distance from the president and chairman of the board was a decided advantage, since he was extremely cautious in not becoming too intimate. However, Hawley Simpson was never sufficiently identified with them to become highly trusted. Trust is not as much of a problem at the lower levels, because the area of administrative freedom is restricted.

It is not uncommon for presidents, especially if they have to assume the role of board chairman, to wish to trust completely any replacement. Some presidents feel difficulty in admitting that this intangible quality is really what they look for in their choice of replacement. The president in Hawley Simpson's case was convinced that unless his replacement could be trusted, he should not be allowed to run a large corporation with the vast amount of power available to him.

Hawley Simpson was passed up for a man who had less organizational genius. This everybody agreed upon. But the wound had been struck and it now bled profusely. His whole administrative style had been predicated on reaching the top by developing superior organizational acumen. Hawley Simpson was not content to be in a staff position the rest of his administrative life. The repressed hostility and fear toward authority figures activated open distrust and hostility toward the new president. His emotional distance grew. Soon he found little interest in even chatting with the boss about relevant responsibilities. His preoccupation grew to absurd proportions; he saw all kinds of dangers ahead for the corporation, many of which could not be substantiated. His judgment became compulsively fixed on a few overworked notions. This rigidity cramped his effectiveness.

Although Hawley Simpson was removed by the president and given less crucial problems, actually the president hoped that Hawley Simpson would work out his difficulties. Instead, Hawley became worse, openly hostile toward the executive group from which he was disenfranchised. The interpretation of this act of exclusion unlocked a barrage of unreserved anger at the president. A verbal scuffle was terminated by the suggestion that Hawley take some time off to relax and get hold of himself. Later, when he was calm, the president said, "You are too valuable to be lost to us. We need you, but you don't seem to need us." Hawley Simpson did not want to leave, fearing what would happen during his absence.

However, he was encouraged by several close colleagues to go away for a month. Hawley set out with his wife and daughter for the Bahamas, only to return three days later in an acute state of panic. In the course of his case analysis, it was discovered that he had not really known or enjoyed his college-age daughter before. Her presence made him feel extremely guilty and pressed upon him an even greater need to succeed. Hawley rushed back to throw himself into the task, the success of which alone could justify his failure with his daughter. During the first afternoon back, he had an acute attack of indigestion. This made him extremely concerned about his health. His work pattern showed definite signs of withdrawal and resignation. He spent unusual amounts of time with his daughter, much to the growing displeasure of his wife. He gave unstintingly of his energies and emotions to his concern for his health and his daughter. Finally, the president urged him to seek administrative counsel. Hawley was directed to the author, who, with the aid of a psychiatric colleague, helped him to recover his usefulness.

Hawley's case illustrates a common executive difficulty—how to develop and maintain positive but moderately reserved attachments to authority figures. Men who cannot maneuver moderately close to superiors without losing detachment and independence usually evidence a deep fear and distrust of authority figures. These men incur distinct disadvantages. Too much fear and distrust will prevent executives from learning from superiors. They will not become effectively integrated with their superiors' work. The dominant notion of authority among successful executives involves activities and people in the milieu outside the executives own management situation. The successful executive feels a part of a wider, more final authority system from which he gains resources and opportunities to act. Authority figures are viewed as helpful rather than destructive and prohibiting. Mark Whiting viewed superiors as dangerous persons, as unstable and unpredictable. They appeared beyond his powers of control. This fear orientation prevented Mark Whiting from respecting, utilizing, and aiding his superiors in a manner customary among executives at the top.

Will Fowler had the same fear orientation that Mark Whiting had. However, he came under the influence of protective, considerate, and wise Mr. Hand. From foreman in the foundry to vice-president of operations, Will Fowler followed in the wake of Mr. Hand. He really had no other superior. And, then, Mr. Hand was not a threatening type of authority figure. Rather, he was viewed by Will Fowler as a kind of brother. More accurately, Fowler and Hand considered themselves to be colleagues.

The disarming and supportive nature of Mr. Hand was exactly what Will Fowler needed to allay his fears and doubts about authority figures. Mr. Hand's failure to nominate his protégé shocked Will Fowler and reactivated his latent fear and doubts about authority figures. He felt that he had been heartlessly betrayed. He vowed that he would never get trapped by personal friendship again. He would become chief executive officer and dissolve all opposition. Then he would make AFEC a leading firm in the country. Note how he reasoned that his corporate objective could be accomplished only after he had acquired unopposed authority and power. This is one of the twists of the mind that sets the authority-centered executive apart from others. Achievement is made possible largely through the acquisition of authority. The achievement drive is easily thwarted or irrationally directed in direct proportion to the lack of authority or the threatening nature of authority figures. Achievement and authority are peculiarly related. Will Fowler resolved to solidify his authority and power base before he proceeded to launch his modernization program. To him, achievement is a consequence of authority. Without authority there can be no effective basis of management.

Because authority is a nuclear value around which the whole management process becomes organized, it is not easy for an authority-centered executive to delegate authority. Something that is prized and eagerly sought is not freely given away. Authority centered-executives reserve the major decisions for themselves and delegate the minor and trivial responsibilities. Mr. Hand practiced this as did Will Fowler. The consequence was that Mr. Hand acquired the major experiences. Will Fowler practiced upon routine and minor responsibility and, in turn, never developed his subordinates for major responsibility either. The problem is that the subordinate is ill-trained for the job ahead and must learn how to perform after he is promoted to the above position. Mr. Hand and Will Fowler made the rungs in the corporate ladder too discrete and independent of each other rather than overlapping.

Authority has a number of symbolic representations. Beside

the delegating of major responsibility, imparting knowledge and information is an authority routine. This is not easily done because it detracts from the superior's reservoir of authority and power. In practice, subordinates are informed only in order to do their work. Requests for additional information are held suspect. Little knowledge is divulged of the superior's problems and responsibilities. Movement into his position is a leap into the unknown for which there is little preparation. Will Fowler felt the unsuspecting stresses and strains of the presidency with little advance warning. The previous rung had not prepared him for the top rung.

The Case of Alvin Peck *

The cases of Mark Whiting, Will Fowler, and Hawley Simpson represent the central problem of authority-centered executives; namely, no one taught them how to properly respect and trust authority figures. The case of Alvin Peck illustrates an authority-centered pattern involving too much respect and affection for authority figures. Alvin Peck's case is represented in Diagram

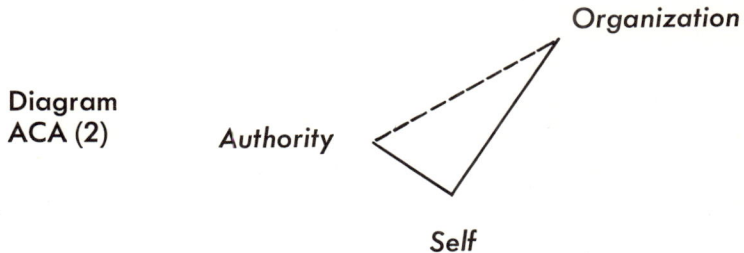

Diagram ACA (2)

ACA(2). This authority-centered pattern reflects a close identification with the authority system and its chief magistrate, the boss (A-S). Like Hawley Simpson, Alvin Peck was moderately identified with the goals and policies, procedures and rules of the corporation. His corporate loyalty was also moderately positive and reserved, as is commonly found in successful executives. He was known as a good company man and cheerfully took on new assignments. However, Alvin had naive trust in superiors and, unlike most executives, had no emotional reservations about them. He had put his high achievement drive in the complete service of his authority set, particularly the boss himself. He had never really defied authority or stood up to it when reasons were available and could not, even if he were prodded. Alvin Peck was completely trusted by every boss during his steady but unspectacular rise through the corporate system. He became the executive vice-president and, as such, really acted as a gatekeeper to the president. Through his office, Alvin Peck allowed to pass only those people and ideas that were relevant and important to the president.

For ten years Alvin Peck had carefully modeled himself after the president. He had learned from him how to make decisions, to communicate, to veto, to delegate. Through the president he had learned how to create the necessary myths and represent needed explanations of why things happened that could not be explained by facts. The corporation had come alive in him as the exact duplicate of the president's version. He and the president were as one. (Alvin Peck occasionally slipped and referred to this relationship as "we.") Other members of the executive team came to rely upon Alvin for decisions which he could make with the boss' assent. Alvin could so well predict the boss' judgment that he would fudge his own decisions as the boss'. It was expected that he would succeed to the presidency.

After the chairman of the board died, the president, at the next meeting of the board of directors, had himself and Alvin ratified as chairman and president, respectively. After the annual meeting, which put the formal stamp of approval by a voice vote, the chairman went to Africa on a six-month hunting trip. Three months later Alvin became known as "table it Alvin." He could not make a difficult decision. Problems would pile up, and when they got so high Alvin would finish them off in one night in rapid fire succession. Many proved to be bad decisions, a fact which made Alvin Peck all the more hesitant and anxious. One very bad decision had to do with a pricing policy that placed the company out of effective competition with their rival firms. The furor from the board and significant stockholders could not be countered by the now timid, weak Alvin Peck. He made the unpardonable administrative sin—he got the board active. The president had what appeared to be a heart attack. Medical authority declared a failure of heart functioning due to extreme fatigue. The chairman came rushing back and assumed the title of chief operating officer. Hearing this while in the hospital, the president made an unexpectedly quick recovery, much to the amazement of his physician and colleagues. Alvin Peck assumed his position as gatekeeper and showed his usual presence and judgment. Five years later, both chairman and president retired, "happy together ever after."

Peck, Simpson, and Fowler Compared

Alvin Peck's case illustrates the crisis that may ensue when a subordinate becomes merely an extension of the boss. Without firm, personally acquired, and authorized notions of self, he had nothing inwardly to rely upon when the boss left. As the image of the boss and how he behaved grew dim, his problems grew big, pushing him into an acute state of anxiety that eventually arrested his administrative style. This style was completely revived upon the return of his beloved boss. The boss' power became his until retirement.

Alvin Peck's case also shows how inadequate or improper emotional identification with authority figures eventually became generalized to include inadequate determination of organizational policy. Feeling inwardly weak without the omnipresence of the power figure, Alvin could not trust his own decisions. His acquired notions of self were borrowed and not personal. This constituted his corporate triangle. False notions of self acquired from overly strong attachments to an authority figure resulted in inadequate administration of corporate goal-setting and policy formulating.

Alvin Peck needed authority every bit as much as did Hawley Simpson and Will Fowler. But he needed the effects of authority, whereas the latter two needed authority itself. Alvin Peck wanted unconsciously to be close to the center of authority, to be protected by it, but a party to it in a passive sense only. He wanted to be accepted by men of authority but wanted them to keep the powers themselves. Will Fowler was vulnerable in this way, too. But his vulnerability was a very precise and limited kind. There are probably very few men who could relax Will Fowler's drive for total power. In this way Mr. Hand's appearance and manner appealed uniquely to Will Fowler's unconscious needs. But what is a very limited vulnerability in Will Fowler becomes a general condition of existence for Alvin Peck. His type goes through life seeking a strong father figure but never really wanting to supercede him. In a way, he wants to remain an obedient, loving son. The thought of becoming his superior's replacement without the latter's presence and support is treated as alien and threatening. If moved into the lonely, isolated position of corporate president, he is very apt to come unglued. Alvin Peck's recovery followed rapidly upon the return of his superior. It is interesting to note that his superior appeared to be authority-centered, but of Hawley Simpson's and Will Fowler's type. Because he did not submit to professional help, the author does not know if this assumption is correct. However, it is entirely plausible. Oftentimes, the Will Fowlers and Hawley Simpsons go for the Alvin Peck type of subordinates. They like submissive, deferential subordinates who willingly accept any task and consider none too menial. Since they enjoy aggressively dominating their subordinates, they may do so without fear of guilt or reprisal because the Alvin Peck types enjoy aggressive domination. There are few superior-subordinate combinations that exude as much mutual admiration. Although this twosome often moves to the top, they are not without vulnerability. A career crisis may develop because the superior imprudently exceeds the boundary of his authoritative rights and the subordinate refuses to utilize his opportunities and rights afforded by the authority of his office. If the superior's upward mobility becomes arrested, too strong of an identification with him usually causes career crisis for the subordinate, too. But the corporate ladder is no respecter of these subtle differences between crisis-stricken men. It is capable of transporting both authority-centered types back down to lower levels in the corporate hierarchy.

6

THE UNBELIEVER AND THE CORPORATE CONSCIENCE

The process of becoming an effective executive involves bringing notions of self and superiors into a meaningful, unified relationship within the goal-achieving activities of the corporation. This suggests that notions of authority are closely tied to notions of organization. The notion of authority held by the successful executive involves belonging to a larger order or system of power and prerogative. Obviously, an elementary notion of authority includes the right to order certain kinds of behavior, not just any or all varieties. There are bounds to authority, and a major boundary is supplied by the explicit and implicit purposes for which the authority system is established. Thus, a boss is expected to authorize behavior that is organizationally directed and relevant. In fact, his main task is to show the relevance of his commands to the goals and purposes of the organization. By definition this task is rational authority. Irrational authority involves commands to be obeyed without showing their clear, convincing relationship to corporate objectives and welfare.

The Organizing Drive

What constitutes the conventional notion of organization in its most elementary form seems to be interconnectedness. Our society is highly equipped today to teach children that the universe is orderly and intricately tied together. In this sense, organization essentially means that everything is or, in some way, can be interrelated. This notion of organization allows individuals to relate to each other and to place a high value upon the products of interaction.

The research of psychologists with children is particularly instructive here. The infant's point of view is that he is the center of the world. A baby, happily watching the movements of his feet, gives the distinct impression of the joy felt by commanding the world. When the baby takes delight in movements situated in the outside world, such as the movements of the ribbons on its cradle, he must feel an immediate bond between these movements and his delight in them. At this stage of infancy, everything participates in the nature of, and can influence, everything else. Activity becomes possible because what the baby does has its counterpart in responses from others and things. The infant grows into childhood with the confidence that events cause other events to happen, that the world is not without sequence, and that there is an essential amenability to human and physical manipulation. Because of this sequential aspect of events, the child can become an event himself and, thereby, participate in the affairs of the world. Because every act is seen to have a potential consequence, the child can order his behavior around anticipated consequences. Goal-directed behavior gradually replaces random behavior. He increasingly organizes his behavior by setting goals and determining their efficient achievement. Others are later seen as capable of entering into this organizational process, and the child's activities become expanded to include the goals and activities of others. He achieves the capacity and skill to play the games of others and, later in life, to work for their goals as though they were his own. From early infancy the child becomes gradually organization-prone. He acquires the belief that all things are in a way connected, or may be connected, by the insertion of a human act of will.

In short, through the agency of the home, the child learns the elementary process of transaction, which involves giving and receiving, making demands upon others, and submitting to others' demands. The notion of taking a role and assuming a position within a group serves to provide the youth with a capacity to perform highly specialized jobs and tasks as well as to become properly equipped for them in adulthood. When the young man appears at the employment office, he is prepared to perform limited roles and to seek great satisfaction in their proper achievement.

Essentially, his notion that things must be organized around particular ends allows him to identify with the ends and goals of the enterprise as they are represented to him at his station or position. These more immediate ends or goals become the means whereby the promising young manager learns to bring things together and perform elementary administrative tasks. The notion of an essential interconnectedness among events and things and the affirmative desire to organize makes practical an identification with the corporation as a goal-achieving activity. Through sustained work performance and upward advancement, the goals of the firm take on more precise meaning. Continually adjusting one's behavior to the demands of efficient organization, as measured by the achievement of corporate goals, produces a positive affirmation of the corporation itself. The executive and the corporation eventually come to be emotional counterparts.

In successful executives the dominant crystallization of the attitude toward organization is the need to take seemingly isolated events or features and see relationships that may tie them together. They often talk about their ability to bring order out of chaos. In short, they like to organize efficiently. What is not said is the obvious. To look for relationships between things and events calls for an underlying notion that there is an essentially possible interconnectedness. This notion of an essential interconnectedness allows operating within vast, complicated systems without losing faith that who one is—one's identity—is important and does count. It allows at the executive level a capacity to hold together the parts of a highly changing organization and to confidently restructure the parts when necessitated by the goal-achieving requirements.

This notion of organization as an essential quality of human and physical events allows for the directing of vast amounts of energy into narrow purposeful channels that otherwise might be dissipated. The successful executive works with facts, is direct in his approach to problems, does not get involved in irrelevant details, organizes his thinking, is markedly crisp and decisive, makes up his mind, and follows through to a solid and definite conclusion. Furthermore, the successful executive is so oriented toward the idea of an essentially possible interconnectedness among things and events that he often overorganizes his environment and himself. Even though some situation arises with which he feels unfamiliar and is unable to cope, he still forces an organization upon it. Thus, he brings it into the sphere of familiarity. This tendency operates partially as a mold, as a pattern into which new or unfamiliar experiences are fit. The executive has a strong tendency to rely upon techniques that will work and to resist situations which do not really fit this mold. The executive is prepared to identify emotionally with the organization and goals of the corporation.

This means that at the top the executive does not think separately of the interests of the stockholders, the employees, and the customers. On the contrary, this executive thinks of the interests of his corporation as a whole. The corporation exists as a total psychological reality which is basically the essential interconnectedness of the many interest groups that press claims upon the executive. It is this organization or interrelatedness of these claimant interests that give him his concept of the corporation. To this concept, he attaches his notions of self. The result is that he thinks and acts as if it were his corporation, even if he has no ownership share in it. When the corporation achieves success, the executive enjoys satisfaction. Deterioration of the firm causes genuine worry, regardless of how his own position is affected. It is interesting to speculate that executives today enjoy more autonomy because of emergence of meaningful identification with corporate goals alongside authority expectations. Executive authority is more rational because it is justified more on the basis of the objective necessities of efficient corporate goal achievements and less on the rights of command.

The development of organization-minded executives does not occur in a vacuum. Some one or group must initiate and reinforce this form of identification. This is where the superior comes in. The executive is not simply a corporation or organization-centered man. He must also be very cognizant of the role of personal, unmediated authorities. He must today be every bit as cognizant of authority figures as was the executive at the turn of the century. Unlike the latter, today's executive must also assume a high identification with the corporation as an entity. In short, the executive's psychic center of gravity pivots around two forms of awareness: authoritative and organizational. But there is still one more base upon which executive identity develops. It is the expectations that the executive levies upon himself in addition to those placed upon him by the requirements of authority and corporate goal achievement.

The Case of Oscar Hanson *

Occasionally, these three corners of the corporate triangle get out of whack. A centering on one angle creates an imbalance in the executive's style of managing. Hawley Simpson and Alvin Peck represent two opposite versions of the authority-centered imbalance. We next turn to two opposite versions of the organization-centered imbalance.

Notice must be given to the relative length of distance between the self and the organization in the OCA(1) pattern. Here the self is felt to be emotionally distant from the goals, policies, rules, regulations, and achievements of the corporation (S-O). The self is felt to be at a medium distance from authority figures and the authority set.

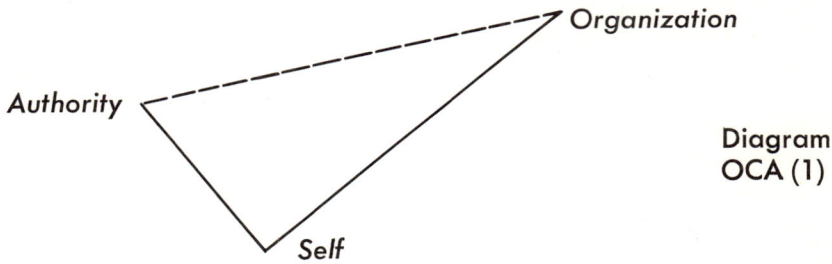

Diagram OCA (1)

The typical mobile executive identifies with the boss but holds a moderate amount of reserve; Oscar Hanson's authority relationship seems to be typical or normal for a successful executive. Because he was not overly attached, he could, if necessary, express clear and meaningful acts of autonomy. However, Oscar Hanson failed to internalize the corporate system as his own. He successfully held off investment of self in the corporation's goals, policies, and achievements. Consequently, he was free to take them or leave them.

On the surface, Oscar Hanson could pass for a professional administrator. Given the goals, he could administer any organization. However, he had a basic weakness. There was nothing really sacred to him. The traditions and precedents built up over a fifty-year period of corporate existence and growth were not respected by him as they were by those who identified more closely with the corporation. This inner freedom to violate easily and unanxiously did not seem to be disadvantageous to him. He was privately proud that he was not an organization man. Valued notions of self were based largely on being an admirer of authority, but not a devotee of man-made institutions such as this corporation. He showed considerable objectivity in a situation where others were partial to the acquired wisdom and achievements of previous corporate officials. To the members of Oscar Hanson's executive group, several past presidents were demigods. The beliefs and values of these heroes of the past were frequently cited and frequently distorted for winning petty arguments. There were offices named for them, chairs at great universities endowed in their names, a philanthropic foundation established in the name of one of them. Even today, many years later, the corporation is still the length and shadow of the illustrious heroes of the past. Few rise to this executive group who do not incorporate the values and beliefs of these heroes.

In the minds of all members of the executive group, except Oscar, the corporation had become a meaningful, symbolic representation largely through identification with these past giants. The current president is a living shrine to them, his office a museum, his home a replica of the past great. There are many totems erected to the prestige and greatness of this tradition-directed corporation. One taboo prohibits smoking in the board of director's room, around the walls of which are hung portraits of the demigods. In this room no one is allowed to raise his voice above the sedate, serene level of near inaudibility. Dress is always in subdued tones and traditional style is never violated. We could continue to show how the firm today is deeply rooted in the past.

Inwardly Oscar was a totally unadulterated maverick. He used to laugh silently at all of this ritual and ceremony. When he wanted to become president, he did not dare to laugh, even privately to himself. His great ambition was to move the corporation out of the "dark ages" and into the blinding light of the roaring mid-fifties. Oscar could not wait to break the taboos and crush the totems. Carefully, he cultivated a repertoire of eulogisms, but they were not really believed. If he was careful, respectful, and patiently loyal, he believed he would become the next president.

In a solemn occasion, marked by no change at all in emotion and expression, the president nominated Oscar for the presidency during the annual board meeting. In this majestic oak paneled, nineteenth-century-style boardroom, he was nominated to the presidency in about the same fashion of forced equanimity that a previous item concerning a minor expenditure was proposed and accepted. The meeting moved on swiftly to the next equally minor affair, approval of the budget that had been in painful preparation since the end of the annual meeting a year ago. Before the meeting was over, Oscar showed his maverick style, and it permanently set the tone of his administration. He dared to get up and express his thanks. This was unheard of, simply because expression of sentiment was frowned upon by members of this great corporation. However, he did speak quietly to the point and the affair was dismissed as unimportant.

With the passage of time, Oscar Hanson showed his disloyalty to the corporate tradition. He proposed a number of new items, most of which were turned down by the board. On one item he invested notions of his whole self: moving the corporation from an essentially manufacturing orientation to a marketing orientation. He began by giving more voice to the marketing people. He identified with their problems, appealed to their itch to become a bigger, better department with more influence. In no time at all, he had a first-class fight on his hands, fought, of course, in the emotionless low key of traditional respect and reserve. Oscar had waited ten years for this struggle, had marshalled his inner reserves well, but the accusation of disloyalty was finally and formally made. The corporate gods had been offended, they cried out for vengeance.

The vice-president in charge of production rose up to accept the gauntlet. Oscar Hanson was now in a struggle that was to last for two long years, during which time neither side was powerful enough to win or weak enough to lose. Oscar came within one vote of ratification exactly one year after the struggle developed openly. It was a defeat of unexpected proportions. Some had betrayed him, other supporters had not acted prudently. Oscar could not back down, not after almost winning. He changed a few arguments and reorganized several features of his marketing strategy to gain lost support. Anything could be arranged—the strategical goals, means, organizational design, and implementation policy. Eventually, all became changed, much to his own detriment. One year later, all support waned. Oscar was revealed as having no really sincere commitments.

In the past, he had never replaced his cynicism with a set of highly valued organization goals and strategies. These were worked out in an effort to continue the sequence of movements toward the presidency. The self never actually became identified with his marketing program. The fight culminated in his being removed as chief executive officer and kicked upstairs as secretary of the board with a decrease in salary.

Oscar Hanson's acute anxiety was not due to his removal. It was, rather, based on shame for having been so well stripped of his masquerade. The ignominy was intolerable. Oscar developed a compulsive desire for self-effacement. He sought love, affection, sympathy, and understanding. He minimized self, inflated others, gave vast amounts of time and energy to finding anyone to support who would support him. Always he took defeat gracefully, since his identification with authority figures was normal and positive. Five years after his solemn nomination to the presidency, Oscar was a confirmed neurotic with a compulsive need for love.

Oscar Hanson's case illustrates the need to believe in something other than authority. The administrative style may become severely distorted by the absence of some firm corporate identification and organizational philosophy. Corporate goals cannot be artificially constructed if others are expected to believe in them. Others will test not simply the feasibility of the goals, but the individual's sincerity. Oscar's sincerity was tested in the peculiar tempo of his traditional-directed firm. Other executive groups may have different ways of testing sincerity. Sincerity stems basically from an identification with the firm, believing in its essential character and not wishing to do violence to it without conviction. The firm was eventually moved into a marketing orbit, with Oscar an inattentive witness seated at a lonely distance from the vital center.

An organization needs a philosophy, a reason for existing, and a set of basic beliefs. The chief formulator and articulor is the president and his executive group. A president like Oscar Hanson is a dangerous threat to any organization. With no philosophy of what should be the normative position of the firm in society, no commitment to a set of highly valued goals, the Oscars could be sold on some goals and purposes that are basically dangerous. With the presidency occupied by one who will not critically examine each and every proposal in the light of an internalized organizational ethic and philosophy, who is to provide this normative function? Oscar failed to replace his cynicism with a personal philosophy of business organization. This form of moral freedom is anathema to the development of organizational integrity and personal responsibility. This kind of behavior is found often enough in clinical case files to suggest that this is a common pattern when one loosely associates rather than sincerely identifies with the organization as a carrier of both a tradition and a future.

The Case of Olaf Johnson *

In the OCA(2) pattern, the executive commits over-identification with the goals and values of the corporation (S-O). He acts very much like the superego of the executive group. As the corporate conscience, he seeks to keep the deliberations and activities of the executive group within the framework of the established objectives, purposes, policies, procedures, rules, and regulations of the corporation. In the past, he has shown strong bureaucratic tendencies. For most executives, the organizational framework anchored around corporate goals and purposes provides a needed guidance and allows them to concentrate upon their achievement and work demands.

Olaf Johnson had always shown a strong disposition to over-identify with roles and procedures in his childhood institutions of

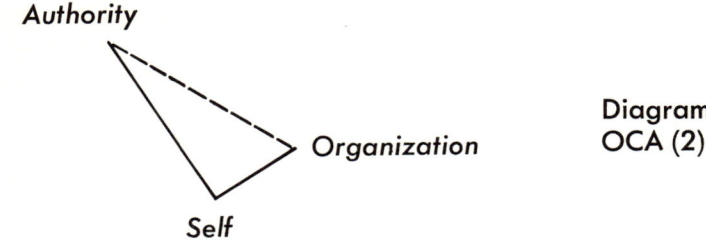

Diagram OCA (2)

home, school, and play. He seemed to excel in the ability to recall all the relevant rules operative to the activity situation. Olaf's history shows a strong emotional attachment to the mother figure, the home, and his home town. He had never really left home emotionally, remaining well attached to the symbols of security and nourishment. He always felt comfortable in well-organized situations and uncomfortable in unstructured ones. His emotional need for order made chess fascinating to him and poker repulsive. In his college courses, his tendency for structure propelled him into the more bureaucratic skills of science as opposed to the humanities. He graduated with degrees in engineering and chemistry with high honors.

In industry he was not an outstanding success as a technician. After several years, he got a job as a management trainee in his present firm. Here he showed a proper identification with the authority system and a sufficiently warm but detached attitude toward colleagues and subordinates. His capacity to work well within the limited confines of lower middle-management brought his superiors' attention. They marked him for a thirteen-week, middle-management training program at a leading university where the approach was very traditional, logical, and methodological in the management and organization subjects. He became well versed in the so-called principles of management and applied them with realistic practicality to the assignments in middle-management positions. He constantly studied the history, precedents, tradition, and rationalizations of the corporation at any given level. He showed a strong ability to perfect existing work systems, pouring vast amounts of self into his organizational routines. He became known for his efficiency and precision, impeccable cleanliness, and fantastic memory. He tended to overorganize managerial assignments. But this was not too distracting to his superiors, since most middle managers in this highly technical chemical firm did not excel at organization.

Only once was Olaf Johnson given an ambiguous, unstructured assignment. The novel situation was threatening to Olaf, but he was extricated by a wise superior who put sufficient boundaries around his responsibility and suggested several important organizational techniques. Olaf and this superior worked so well together that the superior came to rely upon Olaf for his organizational skill. Olaf's close but reserved identification with his superior placed him in good stead, and soon it became apparent that he was going to get a promotion on the heels of his superior's promotion. These two moved together into the executive group when Olaf was forty-six years old. Promotions had left an indelible imprint upon his administrative style. He increasingly realized the high payoff in identifying closely with the corporation. Unconsciously he was engaged in a subtle process of becoming self-immersed in the bureaucracy, traditions, and policies of the firm. Because many in the executive group relied upon him for his expertise, he came to feel a growing sense of importance, far beyond his relative worth to them. The organization as a whole gradually became substituted for other identifications, including those of superiors and subordinates. It became *his* corporation and pangs of insecurity and discomfort occurred whenever people ignored his thorough, precise understanding of policies, tradition, rules, and regulations. Anyone who defied a rule or treated carelessly a policy received his subtle or overt wrath.

The president came to rely heavily upon him. In the slight economic depression of 1958, the executive group entertained some rather drastic ideas. One of these had to do with a complete reorganization of the firm from a product division system to an industry or family of related products divisional structure. Entertaining this drastic change was too much for Olaf. He liked the present structure, had learned to know it better than anyone else. Of course, others expected him to resist. It was obvious that a man so firmly rooted in the corporation system os Olaf would give them a hard time. Olaf mustered his forces well. Others who felt considerable security in the established system supported him. The president and several "young Turks" from marketing and advertising went for the corporate realignment. It was adopted by a majority vote and sent to the whole board for ratification. Olaf saw a last chance to get it stymied. He rounded up several prestigious outside members of the board who placed much faith in his judgment and who liked the system, probably because they were largely ignorant of some of the changes pending in the whole industry. He persuaded four of them to vote against ratification. At the board meeting, the executive group recommendation offered by the president failed by two votes.

To Olaf Johnson, the rape of his corporation had been avoided. However, subsequent events proved that he had merely forestalled the attack upon his corporate mother. It became apparent during the board meeting that those who voted against the recommendation had gotten most of their information from Olaf. The president sensed treachery. It seems that a member of the executive group is not supposed to air his complaints to corporate officials outside of the club. Going to an outside board member was a direct attack on the president, his autonomy and control. Knowing of Olaf's support from the outside board members, the president decided to bide his time and remove Olaf at a future date.

A year later, the president moved against his enemy with the cunning of a fox. He gradually withdrew Olaf's best subordinate by assigning him to a different position that seemed to be well fitted for his competence. Meanwhile, he started a deprivation pattern against Olaf by withholding necessary information and, later, by giving misinformation under the guise of confidence. Next, he promoted Olaf to second vice-president reporting directly to the executive vice-president, a man of strong personality who was one of the last remaining autocratic (i.e., Will Fowler) types. Under Olaf Johnson the president placed another very strong, almost rebellious, executive who was ready for reassignment but who was held on to get into Olaf's hair.

These two executives, a superior and a subordinate, were not sensitive and appreciative of tradition, bureaucracy, and rules and regulations. They had learned to apply them to get the job done and to acquire authority and power. They cramped Olaf in a vise of aloofness and inaccessibility, alternated with authoritarian domination and control. Olaf was constantly at odds with these two who could not be persuaded by Olaf's superior bureaucratic wisdom. To Olaf they were grave threats to the corporation. He set out to crush his subordinate. He was emotionally capable of doing this because, like most mobile executives, he had a typically detached relationship to subordinates in general. Because he had a moderate respect and distrust of superiors that seems very common with executives, he was capable of turning on them, too, when he perceived them to be hostile to his corporation. He turned on both, and out of the struggle his subordinate was removed, but Olaf was transferred to an obviously dead-end position. This movement away from a central position amounted to acute separation from his corporation. Fear and anxiety invaded his whole administrative style, leading to an extreme form of inversion of his affection. Inversion constitutes a withdrawal of the emotional investment, leading to a depersonalization of the object originally identified with.

The corporation gradually grew less and less real and meaningful. He became annoyed at things he once upheld. At times he turned wrathfully upon the very people who had identified with his acts of corporate loyalty. Instability, obstructionism, aggressive humor, and bureaucratic sabotage gradually emerged in his administrative style. He went from bad to worse. His career floundered amidst the corporate rocks where once he had found security and comfort. Emotionally he became mother's bad boy who, disappointed because he could not protect her, decided to attack her. While attending a meeting of business leaders of the chemical industry, he heard of a case similar to his and responded by seeking professional help.

Olaf Johnson's case is clearly one of over-indentification with the corporate figure. His distant, but basically positive, attitude toward authorities allowed him to take them or leave them. What affected his decisions was whether they stood for the same things he did as the active conscience of the corporation. If he had over-identified with authority figures, he could not have rebelled. He would not have gone behind their backs and slit their throats via the garnering of opposition from outside members of the board of directors. The executive group likes to keep the board of directors passive. Olaf activated them and, thus, reduced the autonomy of the executive group. This is an unpardonable administrative sin. He became a threat to them all. The president and the executive group gradually came together in their opposition to him. Even the several members of the executive group who supported him at first saw the necessity and desirability of supporting the president. Olaf became synonymous with board interference and had to be dispensed with. His career crisis is in many respects unique, as are all executives' crises, but it is one version of organizational over-identification.

The important consideration in all of these cases in this book of career crisis is that each executive had a high need to achieve. The life style of each had taken shape early around this important value. Each developed positive notions of self as an achiever and believed he could continually grow in his capacity to achieve. Each showed in the early stage of his career the application of this style to his managerial situation. For each, an administrative style predicated on strong feelings of continued achievement eventually became arrested at some crucial point, causing anxiety. Each executive had the necessary imbalances to cause the arrestment of his achievement drive. In all cases, this arrestment became a crisis of self. The deficiencies became active and mastery of the administrative situation became correspondingly difficult. Thus, high achievers are not perfect, but rather possess imperfections as do low achievers.

Unproductive notions of authority and organization have thus far been accounted for as career crises. These imbalanced notions of authority and organization lead to drastic changes in the self. The whole administrative style becomes out of tune with the reality of the impending danger.

Managing the large business corporation may be pictured as riding a horse that is getting out of rein and growing out from underneath in size at the same time. Our giant firms are getting bigger and more complex. For some, life in the corporation amounts to a test of their capacity to find order when chaos is the rule. In spite of its seeming disorder, the corporation is growing even larger. To some the giant corporation has exceeded the limits of rationality. Their failure to find outlet for the organizational capacities causes frustration of which the acute symptom is often despair. To success-

The Unbeliever and the Corporate Conscience

fully live in such a state of flux and change requires vast amounts of faith in the basic benevolence of organization.

Olaf Johnson's memory of his defeat lingers on five years after he quit this corporation. To salve his badly damaged self-identity, Olaf Johnson has constructed an indictment against big business enterprise. His explanation to leave big business and take up a new career has been wrapped in moral terms in line with his super-active conscience. In his own mind he began to leave the corporation when he began to realize that he was serving no socially worthwhile purpose in helping a giant become even bigger. In speeches he levels his charge against the monster corporations that have the unilateral power to let others live by tolerance only. He paints a gloomy picture of thousands of small subcontractors and distributors existing in a state of peonage to big business, fearful that at any time they may be cut off and annihilated. He indicts the big organization for what it has done to individuals inside. He contrasts the great self-reliance and ambition of the young men of his own generation with the stunted or idealized notions of self of the young men entering the vast bureaucracy of big business today. He describes the warmth of human association found in the small business corporation, wherein corporate goals are felt to be close to performance and achievement. There is, he maintains, utter inhumanity of man toward man when the corporate goals and organization are involved. He states that the absorption of human lives in industrial centralization and in the techniques of less responsible mass movements belittles the individual. The loss of conscience, mutual respect, consideration, and wholesome humanity becomes greater than any possible gain. To Olaf, what large-scale organization leaves out is an essential personal interrelatedness that comes from living out one's life in the company of people who really know each other, deep down, and who, living in one community, usually face together social discipline, integration, and maturity.

Many successful corporation executives will take issue with Olaf Johnson's notions of the malevolence of the big business organization. They will see that they can act within the huge interstices that mark such organizations. Unlike Olaf Johnson, the typical executive feels that he can become a significant element in a complex of forces anchored around goal achievement and organization.

The tendency to feel inadequate and to throw oneself upon the mercy of the organization is found as much or more in the small company as in the large one. What seems clear from the counseling of executives is that an individual without the capacity to seek out the silent opportunities existing about him, whether he is in a large or small grouping, will become threatened by the demands of the organization. This capacity to search hinges seemingly upon the internalization of the belief that the organization is basically helpful to the purposes of self-realization. Without this conventional faith, organizations large or small may become threatening.

Notions of self also spring from within the executive as an active bearer of skills and potentials of achievement. All executives have private notions of what they are and would like to become which are brought to bear upon their performance of administrative tasks. The successful executive has the capacity to express his self-defined needs and desires within the framework granted by the authority system and the corporate ends of the firm. In a way, he utilizes the goals of the firm and the resources made available by the authority system to achieve self-realization. This capacity to achieve self-realization within the corporate framework provides the necessary changes that assure survival and growth. Men like Olaf Johnson, who are only what the corporate system requires, and who take their cues solely from without, are not capable of making the necessary changes that ensure corporate growth and success.

Men like Oscar Hanson, who cannot feel sufficiently attached to the ongoing character and direction of the corporation, are not capable of grasping the essential nature of it and to plumb its deeper meanings and possibilities. The successful executive is capable of feeling attached to the corporation as a meaningful object and of remaining detached so as to be objective. Oscar Hanson and Olaf Johnson failed to have moderate attachment to their corporations.

7

THE PERILS OF THE SELFISH SELF

When a career crisis develops, executives may react in much the same way as people in any other occupation. Their defenses may be no less neurotic, their solutions no less imaginative. They may rely upon normal thinking and activity patterns at a time when something different is required. Or they may resort to radical solutions. They are apt to have unmanageable definitions of their problem and to have exhausted their supply of solutions. Some have severely damaged the most important quality of success and health —notions of security rooted in self-confidence. As the counselor knows, those who doubt themselves tend to doubt the whole world. In panic and desperation the executive comes seeking professional help, but even this is done ambivalently. Guilt and shame prevent easy access to his private inner world. Once penetration of this inner world has been made, his problems are less confusing than the size and complexity of his corporation would suggest. It has always been exciting to notice that the men who manage vast corporations have reduced the workings of the corporate system to a few elementary notions. To be sure, there is more than this suggests to running a business, but in a career crisis, certain boundaries are attached to the administrative process that perhaps do not arise in a normal administrative situation.

Instead of becoming generalized to include other phases of his life style, a career crisis, at least initially, does the very opposite for most. The executive begins to shore up the problem and settle upon a few possibly useful ideas. After all, his main concern is to become or stay meaningfully attached to the administrative process. Separation anxiety haunts the executive who has as his central value the active control of the administrative apparatus of the corporation.

Separation, however, is seldom abrupt and discrete. In the large corporation, the gradual removal of an executive from the central administrative process is seldom perceived by him at the point of its initiation. This is the terror of it all. He feels he is not really pulling his weight, that the tempo is moving against him—but he is not sure.

A number of business practices have developed in recent times to cushion the inhumanity of arbitrary punishment or discharge. The executive may be kicked upstairs, bypassed, gradually frozen out, disenfranchised, or placed on a dusty corporate shelf with problems that never need to be solved. When he has finally confirmed the tragic proportions of the situation, it is almost too late to institute strategic changes. All he knows is that he has done something wrong and somebody in a position of authority has directly or indirectly sanctioned his gradual removal for reasons which may be unknown to him, or which are too threatening to be consciously entertained for long periods of time. Let us continue our journey into the inner world of the executive in a career crisis.

The Power of the Self-Image

In the process of counseling executives in career crisis, some uniformities have evolved that characterize those who come to a psychologist for career guidance. The content of a career crisis involves at least three areas of concern: there is always a problem of authority, a problem having to do with organization, and a problem related to notions of self.

By self, we mean conscious and subconscious orientation to himself as an individual with specific qualities, needs, goals, and values. The answers to the questions, Who am I? Where do I want to go? What do I want to become? are difficult to get from the client. But these answers denote a particular kind of person, what he stands for, what he wants out of life, career, or role.

The self-image of the executive is his psychic center of gravity. In coordination with this psychic center, the two other problem areas come to the fore in a career crisis. Authority involves his orientation toward the initiation of action and the seeking of a superior's consent for that action. The problem of authority may include his activities and that of his superiors' and subordinates'. The problem area of organization concerns performing roles that relate to the goals and values of the corporation, the construction of goals and values that enhance its purposes and policies.

The executive in a career crisis eventually centers his difficulty upon any one or more of these problem areas. He may feel despondent, inadequate, and insecure because he feels incapable of doing what the superior wants or expects of him. He may feel humiliated, resentful, and lonely because he can-not or will not make the sacrifices his corporation expects of executives, superiors and subordinates alike. He may feel aggressive, destructive, and rebellious because he places a higher value upon his abilities and skills than others about him.

These three problem areas are interrelated. They swim around together in the client's stream of consciousness and unconsciousness. For example, executives who suffer from an enlarged view of themselves may reveal some kind of emotional reaction to superiors and to some corporate goal or value. Those who initially reveal a strong distrust of their superiors may reveal images of themselves and their corporation that affect and give form to their suspicions. Executives who find the corporation life impossible may reveal orientations toward self and superiors that bear upon their cynicism or apathy.

Anxiety seems to cause a restriction of the executive's span of awareness. He tends to repress or write off many of the other problem areas in his role and life. He then concentrates on those three to the exclusion of most others. Yet the three are not equally represented in the crisis scene.

Mark Whiting had acquired early in life a problem with the acquisition and exercise of authority and with figures who held superior authority over him. He had acquired the capacity to relate positively to the goals and needs of organized activity. Other executives reported upon in this book have problems that pivot around organization or self. Because these three problem areas are highly interrelated, we are justified in referring to them as forming the shape of a triangle. It is a triangle in which each part depends upon the other two. It is whole or corporate in nature. This means that no one part is relative or useful without the other two. However, in each person one part may outpull the other two in its relevancy to the executive's career crisis. But this predominance of one part is never so complete as to render the other two unimportant.

The key factor to understanding the executive in career crisis is that the *corporate triangle* exists within the mind. Apparently the triangle emerges out of a need to make sense of the career difficulties that stimulate the executive to feel anxious. It helps to define the executive's condition of crisis.

To the individual, reality is what he perceives it to be. He does not act upon what the superior is really like, or his organization, or even his self. Rather, his behavior is based upon what he thinks his boss is like, what he thinks the corporation life demands of him, what he thinks he experiences when he is "being himself." The corporate triangle is subjective and wholly individual.

The outside events and happenings that press forward in a crisis situation stimulate their counterparts in the inner world of the executive. These inner events and happenings may be initially called into operation by the crisis situation, but their specific character and form emerge from the many experiences of the executive throughout his whole life. In this sense, a crisis situation may stimulate the executive to feel that his whole life is at stake. This is an acute career crisis.

In such cases, events and happenings relating to childhood experiences may emerge to vitally affect the way in which the crisis is handled. The aggression brought to bear upon the president who opposed Whiting's selection of a subordinate was greatly increased by the many times in his life when he had been rejected or threatened by authority figures. Few career crises can be understood without ascertaining the relative positions of these notions of authority, organization, and self.

We have thus far accounted for the role of notions of authority and organization in the executive personality. Little has been directly said about self or identity. What an executive is willing or not willing to do in the throes of a career crisis largely depends upon the kind of person he thinks he is. If a career crisis does anything at all, it forces the executive to take a good look at himself. Very few executives ever have an occasion to confront themselves. During relatively tense or critical career episodes, the executive may be aware of a few aspirations, disappointments, and fears. But a sense of continuity and confidence is preserved by this rather fleeting self-analysis. In making judgments and decisions, he uses his same self as the central point of reference, with only a few minor modifications and additions. By this means, notions of self accrue over a long period of time. An executive is thus able to act with reasonable consistency because of the relative stability of his self-conceptions. His superiors and subordinates can rely upon him to act predictably in a wide variety of situations. Regularity, the key to organization, and trust, the key to delegation of authority, are made possible by virtue of stable self-conceptions. Stable self-conceptions are the basis of organized life.

Self-conceptions are also the basis of an executive's career. A career is the manner in which an individual is organized to act with reference to some future destination. This terminal point is not simply a position in the corporation, but a set of personal characteristics and attributes—self-conceptions. Aspiring to achieve these qualities definitely affects his present conduct. Each executive makes sacrifices in order to achieve his career objectives. Mobile executives often suffer through unchallenging work assignments that are worthless to their career designs except as necessary steps to higher objectives. Counseling of executives indicates that as much as two of three jobs are below the executive's notions of self-worth. The public often pictures the top of the corporation as a center of excitement, novelty, and challenge. This is not a correct picture of the executive's life. About eighty percent of a president's time is spent in relatively routine activity. But the remaining twenty percent is self-sustaining and self-invigorating.

Because of high degrees of work uniformity, routine, and regularity, the climb upwards could become exasperating if it were not for the few significant and highly valued rewards at higher positions leading to the top. We have noted the most mobile executives are high achievers. An achievement drive arises out of an individual making conscious designations to himself. He sees himself as being able to master the managerial situation, and his hopes become validated through his achievements. The honor, status, reward, prestige, and affection they bestow or receive are less valued than having their notions of their capacities and skills affirmed by success. To the high achievers, the excitement of challenging work and the self-affirmation that ensues from successful performance is what causes him to mobilize his energy each day throughout his career.

In contrast is the pseudo-achiever for whom the secondary products of reward, status, power are mainly stressed. For him it is not the doing and arriving, but the receiving that is all important. This executive looks to the future in terms of the glory it provides him as opposed to the achieved drive of the other, who looks more to the sheer accomplishment of work itself. Both types—achievers and pseudo-achievers—are found at the top, but clinical experience suggests that the real achiever type is by far predominant.

Utilizing the concept of self or identity, we can make another distinction among executives at the top. Some executives' notions of self are gross projections into the future. They see themselves as capable of mastering jobs or roles much more challenging than their present roles. The self is larger than the present role. The executive experiences himself as overly prepared, not only for his present assignment, but for several that may lie ahead. The opposite type of executive is one who feels inadequate for his present and future assignments. His notions of self are smaller than what his role requires. The latter feels inferior and the former superior. Although it is not definitely known which of the two types is the most mobile, it would logically suggest that the "self superior than role type" would emerge in greater numbers at the top of the corporation. Counseling experience affirms the greater amount of energy made available to the role by an executive who is ambitious. However, the rocky road to the top can become a nightmare of projected threats and fears if the executive does not constantly have his superior notions of self affirmed. A career crisis can emerge from too much ambition improperly and impatiently applied to role responsibilities. The blow of a career crisis can have devastating effects to an executive with grossly superior notions of self. Let us examine this possible effect by means of the case of Sam Cory.

The Case of Sam Cory *

Sam was a supreme egotist who felt infinitely superior to the administrative task. In Sam there never were any conscious doubts that he could become president. Few reservations were entertained about his ability to perform any assignment, if he wanted to. From early childhood, everything he did was to overcome feelings of inferiority. He became compulsively addicted to proving his prowess, mastery, and potency. In his late adolescent sex life, he became a Don Juan, moving from girl to girl to prove he could handle even the most resistant. In aptitude, he had a flair for the dramatic, as though he were always very conscious of each person in the audience watching him. Defeat, stupidity, failure, or inadequate skill brought him to the edge of intense shame. Always he bounced back to prove that he had merely not tried hard enough. He thrilled at glory and bled at failure. In track he outran others, not because he wanted to test his inherent strength, but to prove his superiority. In college he set about continuing his adolescent successes but with greater competitive spirit. The drive for glory was not too great to require him to take account of reality. He measured his rivals, observed their defects, moved against them with the studied zeal of a chess player. He remembered all successes and repressed all failures as quirks of fate, oddities of situation, and peculiarities of people.

His reputation as a big wheel on campus and his high scholastic average made him an attractive candidate for a large corporate managerial training program. He decided, however, to stay for a master's degree, and during this period he married the daughter of a very prominent upper-class family. His successful marriage added to his already idealized image of self. The case files show that this pattern of marriage could belong to any number of self-centered executives.

We next observe Sam in a middle-management training program several years ahead of most men. In the classes, he was extremely quick to show understanding and very facile in asking profound questions. He still had a boyish trait that made him appear to be bright, hungry, but socially immature. His superiors decided he needed grooming and placed him in a very difficult position in the firm. They wanted him to get in over his head and to call for their help, hoping that he could become more cognizant of the need of help from others. He did much worse than they had anticipated, and got into severe trouble. He could not find enough excuses; he implicated innocent persons and defended his own competence. He was thoroughly admonished and sent back to a position several grades lower. He used a trick he had learned in college football. He had sufficient alertness to again study his superiors and the mobile managers around. He realized that they all tended to look positively to their superior for help and supported organized goals and procedures that included others. He developed a pseudo-democratic style, much to the internal anguish of his idealized self. He acquired instrumental identification with authority and organizational objects to enable him to avoid any failure again. While he was working hard and actively releasing energy resources, he was not aware of how emotionally isolated he was from the authority system and from the values and goals of the corporation.

Sam developed an administrative style that took him far up the ladder toward the top. At the age of thirty-eight and in a position commanding a salary of $35,000 Sam had his next crisis. It was extremely unexpected. Basically, it stemmed from misreading the cues of authority figures, a mistake that is common to self-centered executives due to a tendency to be concerned only about self. He was asked to become a special assistant to the public relations director: a staff man to another staff man. This was interpreted as arrestment of upward mobility. Actually, Sam was being placed on a temporary shelf away from an authority figure who was knifing him behind his back. Sam had never been told of this treachery, or that he was to be reactivated as soon as possible. To say this might reveal a respect for him that his superiors felt was not yet completely justified. Yet, they saw great things ahead for Sam and, for this reason, took him out of incipient trouble.

Sam's idealized self prevented reading these cues. He immediately took flight and accepted a position in a competitive corporation that always needed junior executives and evaluated highly those developed by Sam's corporation. He received a substantial promotion as sales manager for the whole corporation, reporting directly to the vice-president of marketing. This spectacular rise enhanced his long-standing conviction that he could do anything and the top was merely waiting to receive him. The members of his corporation extracted valuable ideas from him, which he had obtained from his experience in the previous corporation. He felt big and important and manufactured as much information as he had actually obtained.

Luck entered the picture at this point. The marketing executive sent his key subordinate to the Continent to set up a multinational market structure for the sale of the corporation's products abroad. The boss and Sam developed workable relationships by which Sam acquired a great deal of corporate visibility. He could still control his self-centered tendencies to gain information, experience, and support. Suddenly, the marketing executive died of a fast-developing malignancy. The executive group picked Sam because they could not bring the other subordinate back from Europe at this time. They told him he was acting manager of marketing and that the other executive might be given the title of vice-president of marketing upon his return. Determined that no one would dislodge him and that no one could, he pitched into the task of making the opportunity over to fit his career designs. It became increasingly apparent to the executive group that Sam, now forty-three, was immature. They could see what he had in mind and set up blocks when it was strategically desirable. Hemmed in and without permanent portfolio, Sam took to cultivating a few select members of the executive group. He hauled out his prize possession, his well-to-do, charming, sophisticated wife, and used her to penetrate the closed inner circle of executive wives. She did her job well. Because she was basically a nice person, they took to her and, thereby, she and Sam moved into the social world of the corporate system.

All the while, his self-centeredness was beginning to show in his administrative situation, and it began to show now in combination with the social situation. Sam had committed a mistake that egotists, by their very nature, are apt to make. He overexposed himself and, thereby, his idealized self, too. The effect was lethal. The president called for the return of the executive in Europe whose assignment was almost completed. For his own sake and that of the corporation, he was apprised of the situation but not completely informed about Sam. However, one of the prerogatives of a vice-president in the corporation, and in many other institutions, is that he is allowed to select his own crucial subordinates. Believing in this principle, the new vice-president of marketing immediately had Sam's name given to the executive personnel committee for relocation. Sam found the entrance of the returning executive intolerable, his ascendancy to the vice-presidency threatening, and his own transfer unassimilable to his self-respect.

For the first time in his life, Sam felt the pangs of complete isolation and loneliness. Because he had neither emotional identification with authority figures nor emotional identification with the corporation, he could very easily entertain the thought of resigning. He did, and they called his hand. Now his lack of identification with authority and organization brought extreme feelings of anxiety. He was alone for the first time, separated from the instruments of self-glorification. The tailspin was acute and complete. The thought that he had failed could not be entertained by his grandiose self. The others were completely wrong, stupid, foolish for letting such a good man as himself go. All of his achievement, extending as far back as college and high school days, paraded before him in semiconscious review. Of his mistakes, weaknesses, and failings he was not conscious. By means of this review of his past accomplishments, he could not understand how anyone could fail to realize that he was a "big" man. To add to his troubles, his wife was thoroughly embarrassed, as were her upper-class parents. The story he concocted to keep her on his side was a mixture of rationalizations, untruths, and projections all geared more to preserve his idealized notions of self than to preserve her pride. By the time he faced her parents, his story had been told so many times that he thoroughly believed it—and so did they.

With the help of her parents, he acquired the vice-presidency of marketing of a small firm in the upper-eastern region. Having by now a low capacity to respond to reality, he failed to see how incapacitated his idealized self had made him. His weak, hostile administrative style was no longer simply compulsive competitiveness. It became a weapon to destroy others. He appealed to aggression. This appeal involved his whole life style, even his marriage area. He argued with his wife, beat her, and stripped her of dignity and self-respect. She left him and with the children went to her parents. He did not care, for now he could put his whole life into achieving vindication. He manipulated authority figures and conceived attractive goals for the organization. He charmed, wined and dined, pushed, retreated, and complied all for one purpose—complete and total success and vindication. He got several stockholders and a banker to put up money for enough stock to gain control of the corporation. At the age of fifty, Sam became the president. However, under his maniacal direction the corporation went steadily downhill. When the capital assets became substantially greater than the value of the stock, a giant corporation bought the majority stock out from under him. He was absorbed into the big corporation as a member of the board of directors because of the large block of stock that he owned and controlled. But because of his record as a poor president, he was given no administrative post.

The case of Sam is one of isolation and loneliness. A real emotional cost is paid for incapacity to relate positively and meaningfully to authority figures and to corporate goals and values. Sam is a rebel whose cause is himself and whose glory is in the complete and total defeat of others. To all ordinary appearances, Sam is today a man of position. His initial investment of $100,000, partly borrowed and partly acquired from savings, is now worth about two million in stock of the large corporation. He dresses well, drives a fine automobile, makes frequent speeches for the chambers of commerce and trade association groups, and has many acquaintances. He has few close friends, no wife and family, no real identification with society, community, and corporation. Outwardly successful, inwardly he is weak and impoverished. Around the night clubs he is his old Don Juan self. In his church he has now become an elder, and in his political party a loyal champion. He has addressed himself to all the self-enhancing positions in his society. He seeks always to prove his superiority.

Sam is not a man who respects authority or organization. His notions of self make him appear to be bigger and above the laws of human association. It is possible for the self-centered executive to have strong superiority feelings toward either authority or organization. In Sam, neurotic feelings of superiority were directed toward both the authority figures and the goals and values of organization.

[See Diagram SCA(1).] When only one becomes the object of superiority feelings, the administrative situation is potentially less anxiety-creating. The executive may feel vastly superior to the requirements of authority, but his rebellious tendencies may be kept partially in check by his organizational identification. Or his tendency to rebel against the values and goals of the organization may be kept in check by positive identification with the authority figures. The completely self-centered person is a rarity in large business corporations. Usually some internalized respect for authority or organization will keep the idealization-of-self process within more productive and realistic proportions. Sam is an example of an exceptional case.

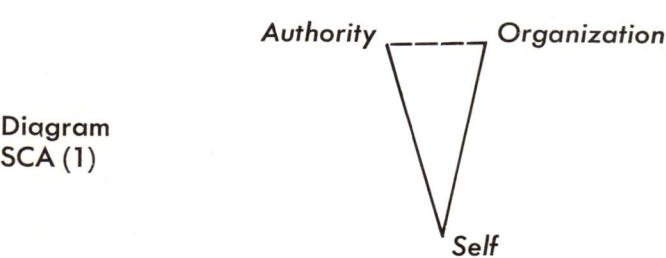

Diagram
SCA (1)

It might seem that self-centeredness runs high throughout the other two basic crisis patterns—ACA and OCA. The executive may show an authority-centered pattern because he is only concerned with self-needs. The authority-centered pattern essentially reflects an overly pronounced concern with the problems of authority and authority figures. This concern may stem either from irrational needs and fears of authority (ACA) or from an enlarged view of self (SCA) that prohibits easy relationships with authority. Likewise, the organization-centered pattern essentially reflects an overly pronounced concern with the problem of organization. This preoccupation may stem from irrational needs and fears (OCA), or an idealized self (SCA), that will not allow adequate integration with organizational realities.

Then, too, it is possible for there is to be self-centeredness that is not accounted for by the emotional possibilities inherent in the other two patterns. In other words, the executive may have notions of self that are unproductive and faulty in and of themselves. His self-definitions are unrelated to the conventional objectives of most executives. Under such circumstances, he views his managerial role as secondary or necessary for the performance of another more meaningful role. Work and the prerequisites of gainful employment merely aid the pursuit of other interests highly equated to his self-identity. He will be in the corporation but not of it.

The Case of Oliver Dansby *

At first glance, the self-centered pattern that views the managerial role as secondary may not seem relevant to a discussion of career failure. How can a man fail in a job that is not highly valued? What possible consequences could enure to the corporation from the failure of an executive to become self-involved in the traditional matters of managerial authority and corporate organization? These questions strike at the heart of the concept of the corporate triangle. In effect, they challenge the necessity of an executive to be at least moderately attached to the goals and purposes of the corporation and to be sensitive to the powers and responsibilities that devolve upon executives at the top.

The case of Oliver Dansby is relevant to these questions. His form of self-centeredness offered little active involvement in the crucial affairs of his corporation. In a moment of desperation, he gave his support to a faction in the corporation. His efforts caused his corporation great harm and set back for sometime a very much needed program of centralization of authority. But Oliver Dansby did not have a logical mind about authority and he was unaware of these grave consequences to the welfare of the corporation. When apprised, he seemed indifferent and inaccessible. Oliver Dansby had not the conscience that stirred ordinary men to commit themselves morally to corporate causes. Fortune mistakenly singled him out to cast the deciding vote for law and order in his corporation. But he voted to ensure his noninvolved pattern of life.

We shall see that there is another form of self-centeredness as lethal to corporate ends as that of Sam Cory. But it is a different kind of self-centeredness. It stems not from inflated notions of self that places the executive above the principles of authority and organization, as was Sam Cory's case. Rather, Oliver Dansby was immune to the dictates of authority and organization. He was emotionally outside of the circle of conventional forces of authority and organization. In this sense, his case represents the potentially disastrous effects of a noninvolved, self-centered executive.

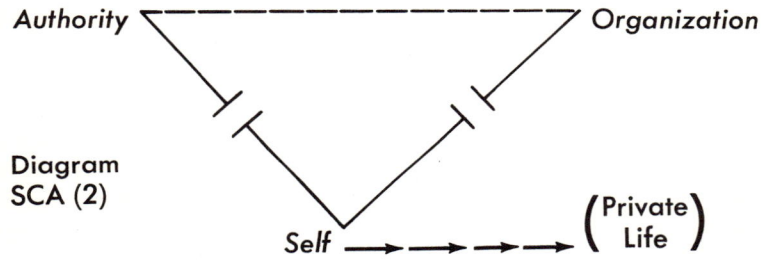

Diagram SCA (2)

In Diagram SCA(2) note the broken lines leading to the authority and organization corners of the corporate triangle. These broken lines represent a detached orientation toward superiors and corporation. The self is directed largely by the attractiveness of goals and objectives anchored in private life. In a way, Oliver Dansby did not have the typical AOS mental framework. The consequences of his unusual mental development reverberated throughout his authority set and threatened the continuity of the whole organization.

Oliver Dansby was one of those rare executives who seldom sought opportunity and success. He never worked for a specific promotion, never schemed to attract attention, never dominated to invite respect, and never charmed to dissolve resistance. The layman would call Oliver an introvert. He was quiet, unassuming, gentle, pleasant, and fainthearted. He dressed conservatively, ate gingerly, and talked reservedly. He had a deep distaste for the spectacular, the profane, and the conspicuous. Yet, he did not fight aggressively against these common characteristics of our modern society. Toward people, he assumed a detached, aloof posture. How he became a treasurer and controller of a large corporation may seem unfathomable to the reader. But what he did as controller was entirely predictable, given his reserved personality.

Oliver Dansby's career crisis began the day his executive group launched a palace revolt against the president. The president, Mr. Kearns, was the chief executive officer of a large industrial corporation that had many different products in its marketing mix. He presided over eight wholly owned subsidiaries. Each president of a subsidiary corporation was a chief executive officer in his own right. The subsidiary presidents were accustomed to wide latitude. Each subsidiary was looked upon as an independent profit-making center. The budget for the whole corporation was a sum of the individual budgets of the subsidiaries plus a budget for the administrative staff of the president. This staff included each of the eight subsidiary presidents and three group vice-presidents. These group vice-presidents were staff men who operated as buffers and liaison officers between the president and the subsidiary executives.

This loosely held federation of semiautonomous subsidiaries worked well in the past. During the early 1950's the corporation was composed of two divisions that served largely the automobile products industry. The desire to acquire a broader, more stable product base led the former president to buy a medium size firm in the airplane parts manufacturing industry. Next, he bought a thriving business in the chemical industry and, then, a prosperous but badly managed firm in the road equipment manufacturing industry. By 1960 the corporation was a kind of holding firm for eight wholly owned subsidiaries. At that time, Mr. Kearns was a general manager of one of the two original divisions. He was promoted because he believed that the office of the president should be as weak as possible, with no powers except those granted him voluntarily by the subsidiaries. The subsidiary presidents believed that the government was best that ruled the least. A staunch Republican both politically and administratively, Mr. Kearns reigned rather than ruled.

Oliver Dansby was his controller when he was president of a subsidiary. When made corporation president, Mr. Kearns made Oliver treasure and controller over the whole works. Since Oliver was competent, pleasant, and unaggressive, he created no enemies, nor friends for that matter, and his elevation to corporate level almost escaped notice by the subsidiary presidents.

In the corporate controllership, Oliver Dansby became unwillingly engaged in a dangerous development. His reports alerted the president to the fact that the subsidiaries were actually working against each other, keeping progress and profits to a dangerously low level. Because the product markets were overlapped, several salesmen from the corporation called on the same client-buyer. As research and development became increasingly necessary, several subsidiaries unwittingly employed scientists and technicians to develop the same product. Each subsidiary's inflated budget reflected the high cost of overlapping sales, research, engineering, and managerial personnel. As a collective entity, this corporation was running out of control, and as a once profitable enterprise, it was running out of capital. Circumstances forced the corporate president to call the executive group together and inquire about what should be done. Being accustomed to autonomy and characteristically strong-willed, the subsidiary presidents had as many answers as they had members on the executive committee. However, no one was willing to grant the president strong, centralized powers of authority and responsibility.

By 1962 their corporate dilemma was still unresolved, with time, money, and markets moving exorably against them. Seeing that the corporation was in grave danger, the president attempted to break the stalemate and asked for dictatorial powers for the period of the emergency. His strategy called for winning over at least two of the subsidiary presidents. He assumed that they and his executive staff could shout down the remaining subsidiary presidents.

He took three months to win the support of the two subsidiary presidents, but failed to devote any time to informing his own staff and gaining their tacit acceptance of his plan. He assumed that since they served at his request, they would approve his program. He misread the intentions and character of Oliver Dansby, his corporate controller. Actually, Oliver Dansby had never taken up the sword for his own protection or for the fight of another.

During his rise to the corporate level, he was completely unscathed by any feuding and fighting.

Unlike the other members of the corporate executive group, Oliver Dansby did not start at the bottom. He became a certified public accountant when he graduated from college and joined a large public accounting firm. His rise in the firm to a junior partner was unspectacular, since the rule was that after ten years he would either go up or out. He went up simply because he had no enemies. His lack of friends did not hurt him. Although he had only adequate technical competency, he had the capacity to get the right people and talent engaged with a client account. He gradually developed what on the surface appeared to be a democratic style of management. At that time, his permissive style seemed refreshing to his superiors and to the practice of public accounting, and he was given bigger and more prestigious accounts. He never eagerly sought these promotions and, if anything, he showed reluctance to accept them. His permissive, unassuming leadership made him appear fit for junior partnership. His superiors, the managing partners, did not know that he had little ambition and aggressiveness. They merely assumed that he had these qualities in great strength but held them in check, much as they had done during their climb up the corporate ladder. Little did they suspect that Oliver Dansby got others involved in his work because he was constitutionally lazy.

Oliver Dansby did not really want to make much of a career for himself. The achievement drive that parents so assiduously developed in their children escaped him. His parents were highly educated people of secure middle-class background. His father was a professor of Greek history at a very conservative and small eastern college. His mother held a doctorate degree and never had to worry about money or security of any kind because she was brought up by academic parents who found in philosophy, ideas, and arguments their central values of life.

As a boy Oliver Dansby was close to his mother and father. They were very permissive and did not practice the authoritarian rule as did most middle-class parents at that time. The home was never orderly (in fact, it was always a mess) and the father never dominated. Oliver went to a private prep school that was basically indulgent and paternalistic in its educational policy. He chose his father's college to get his bachelor's degree and he majored in accounting to ensure some means of livelihood. Because of these circumstances, he was protected largely from the effects of the vigorous assertion of the success ethic that undergirded the rest of society. Being the only child, he was spoiled rotten by generous portions of love and kindness. He never heard an angry voice in his home nor felt the firm consequences of arbitrary authority. He never looked upon his father as an authority figure and never had to assume a work role in the home. Consequently, he never had the usual superior-subordinate hierarchical frame of reference or an instinctive respect for organization and order. Since his home life was one intellectual experience after another, he needed little academic exposure of the type afforded by college education. For this reason he chose accounting without any lengthy deliberation. Although he did not relate to most of his instructors, he found in accounting a basic neutrality from the intense intellectual arguments that frequently occasioned his home life.

Oliver was a brilliant student, but not in the academic classroom. He loved to read the books that comprised his mother's and father's libraries. He was an avid student of the great books and of great men of history. In college he showed a complete affirmation of a sedentary life. He did not like competitive sports or group sports of any kind. He liked reading, painting, and poetry. Occasionally he played chess, but enjoyed more the reading about chess and of great men of chess. He loved the life of his family and embraced his intellectual heritage vigorously.

Because his life in the home with his parents and their friends, with his private hobbies and interests, drained much of his daily energy, he found in the academic classroom and in accounting momentary pause and relaxation. Accounting served as a prelude to his intellectual life at home. Because he was bright, he did not have to work hard to get his grades. At his college a gentleman got C's and occasionally B's. Only a boor got A's. Oliver Dansby proved to be a gentleman. His day usually sprang to life after he left his classrooms. This, then, was the routine that would stamp Oliver Dansby for life. As a dedicated intellectual, he assumed a detached, noninvolved orientation toward all things striking of career and work.

How, then, did he get a certificate of public accounting? It can be explained by a momentary flirtation with ambition. He found one instructor whom he liked and was encouraged by him to sit for his C.P.A. exams. This was one of the few times that he ever was challenged. During the course of this year of preparation for his state exams, he acted out of character to his parents. He spent hours at the library going over books and exam questions. He showed uncommon amounts of persistence, concentration, and commitment. He passed his C.P.A. exam with honors. He was a Gold Medal winner. Thereafter, his energy level fell off and his short flirtation with worldly success ended. He assumed his former pose toward life. Said Oliver Dansby, "I proved to myself that the 'bitch-goddess of success' was made easily . . . that the specific goals and objectives that society sets for the young are transparently false. They call out technique, not wisdom. . . . The individual is reduced in quality and dignity to the level representative of his crass achievements." One can see the intellectual bent of his developing mind. To Oliver Dansby work was the means of acquiring the necessary resources to gain his highly intellectual ends. He existed during the day so he could revel in the great literature late into the night.

A large public accounting firm discovered his examination score and offered him an attractive career. He accepted reluctantly and inwardly he aspired to no permanent career. When he was made a junior partner, he had his second short flirtation with the crass trappings of the "bitch-goddess of success." For a period of three years he employed vigorously his permissive, democratic style to manage the small staff assigned to help him with his accounts. In 1957 he handled the account of Mr. Kearn's subsidiary corporation. In this capacity he came to the attention of Mr. Kearns who offered him the job of controller. He accepted without relish or thanks. Because of the salary and security provisions, he decided that he now had more than the financial resources necessary to pursue his private intellectual career. Once again the full power of his mind reverted to his private life. He said, "I ran the division controllership out of the back of my pocket." He withdrew psychologically from his work career.

Oliver Dansby never married. He remained a close, loving son until his parents' death. He did not enjoy children or constant company of any kind. He could win friendship when he chose to and accumulated several lady friends, half of whom were married. However, these friends always had one thing in common—they were intellectuals. Although he had his share of sexual affairs, he never let his life pivot on his sex needs. He said, "Sex and work are the same: they are necessities of life."

When Oliver Dansby assumed the position of corporate controller, he saw the future as secure and benevolent. He was then only thirty-five years old. He carried out his duties in craftsmanlike manner, always maintaining detachment and poise, graciousness, and firmness. He never got involved with anyone, issued his statements in precise, impersonal terms that fitted the objectivity and candor of the accounting principles and functions. He used numbers, percentages, and accounting jargon both to supply answers and to remain uninvolved.

Suddenly, his serene life was shattered by the attempt of the president to assume dictatorial powers. Mr. Kearns needed the facts and figures made available by the accounting function. But he needed even more urgently the loyal support of the controller. For Oliver Dansby, this was impossible to expect. His whole approach to work was one of personal non-involvement. He would so act to maintain his detachment. Instead of supporting the president, he took what for him was the lazy way out. He announced to all members of the executive committee that the corporate interests would be best served if the controller made his knowledge and reports available to all members equally. He believed that if the controller did not assume absolute neutrality, the financial state of the corporation would be misconstrued in accordance with his allegiances. He said, "Numbers are neutral in essence and those who devise their meanings should be neutral." With this statement of service and objectivity, Oliver Dansby unknowingly placed his president in grave danger. Now the president would have to convince three subsidiary presidents to vote for his program of centralized authority and power. Persuading a third subsidiary president was considered impossible. Keeping the two in his corner became increasingly difficult because of Oliver Dansby's announced neutrality. Others sensed that the president was making a grab for power for the sake of self-aggrandizement and sought every opportunity to use Oliver's neutrality for what had become their moral duty to remove the power-hungry president.

Oliver's life of noninvolvement became filled with bitter disappointment. The requests made by members of both camps were ambiguous, biased, and hostile in intent. At first, he thought he would be a mere appendage to the highly computerized accounting system and profer facts and figures mechanically and impartially. Soon he discovered that they were distorting his data and information and seeing behind them intentions that he felt did not exist. He realized that he could not continue for long his neutral role without losing his integrity. The more he listened to the interminable arguments of the executive committee, the more he felt trapped. The arguments lingered in his ears long after he returned to the sanctuary of his home life. They were disturbing him where he thought no worldly affairs could penetrate—his intellectual fortifications.

Oliver Dansby became deeply unsettled by the power hungry cries of these passionate men, not because they were passionate, but because they interfered with his private interests. His protected life had not prepared him well to cope with what he called "these corporate gladiators." He felt like a Christian on the floor of a Roman amphitheater. He tried hard to soften the din by reading Carlyle and Emerson, but they and a host of his favorite poets, philosophers, and humanists failed to work their magic. In anguish he decided to defend the invasion of his privacy and yielded to the incessant pressure applied to him by the militant members of both camps. Oliver Dansby believed that the whole crisis would dissolve if he added his voice and vote to one of the belligerent groups. He cast the majority vote for continuing the corporate form of federation. He voted against the president, who was the last to suspect his disloyalty. He did so because this was the best way to stabilize the corporate ship again. The president felt betrayed, pleaded that Oliver maintain his neutrality at least. But Oliver was not brought up with the traditional notions of authority. He did not feel the pangs of conscience when he turned on his superior. Nor did he have a strong urge to identify with organizational needs and necessities. It was not that he was fearful of authority or distrustful of large organizations. He was simply without these conventional orientations. He remained unmoved. Finally, the president came to Oliver's home to plead that he change his mind. His arguments for the need for centralized authority and the corporation's need for systematic planning and organization did not reach Oliver. He saw these terms and orientations as simple contrivances of human ambition.

However, the president captured a rare glimpse of Oliver Dansby. His massive library, the opened, well-used books on his desk, and the atmosphere of his home in general attested clearly to Oliver Dansby's real character. With this insight, the president queried Oliver about his habits, hobbies, and general interests. He broke through the icy surface of Oliver's appearance to the real man inside—the intellectual. So this was what made Oliver tick. With uncommon skill, Mr. Kearn drew out Oliver from behind his bland facade. Oliver proved vulnerable to the president's faulty but disarming references to such notable giants as Nietzche and John Stuart Mill. Oliver entered into an intimate, four-hour discussion of his many intellectual interests. At a very late hour the president broke off the discussion by a reference again to the corporate scene and Oliver's moral role. The icy cast of detachment and imperturbability reappeared automatically. The president excused himself and left in a state of despair.

Soon afterwards, the corporate staff was reorganized by the victorious subsidiary presidents. They chose from among them a new president. Oliver Dansby did not escape their corporate maneuvers. Because he had turned on his superior, he could not be trusted by the new president. Fearing that Oliver Dansby was capable of future treachery, the executive group agreed with the president that he be dismissed and granted a year's salary in advance. What was initially meant to restore Oliver's intellectual life, now threatened to destroy the economic base that made his private life possible and enjoyable. He was turned out because of his apparent ruthlessness. What they did not know was that Oliver Dansby fought passionately to keep his private life intact. He wanted nothing that ordinary men fought for. Their conventional aspirations were disgusting; their world of organized living was not real. The true values of life could not be found in the pursuit of profits and power and the advantages they provided.

The new president and his executive group did not understand Oliver Dansby's true character. The ruthlessness that they ascribed to his behavior was their own self-centeredness. Oliver Dansby was self-centered differently. His whole personality pivoted upon maintaining his smug, impersonal, abstract, detached way of life. He conceived of himself as an intellectual who, because of improvidence, consented to earn a living. He was at base just as selfish as each of the men who aspired to replace the president.

However, Oliver Dansby did not see himself as self-centered. When he first came for professional help, his prime objective was to find someone to listen to him and sought in counseling complete self-justification for his noninvolved style of life. His rejection by the corporation reinforced a growing conviction that only in the realm of ideas could one find safety and security. He had been out of work for fourteen months and without any visible means of economic support. Because he had been frugal for many years, he had enough money to live comfortably for several more years. It was gradually revealed that Oliver Dansby did not intend to work ever. Then why did he come for career counseling if he did not intend to work again? Had he not renounced any claim to the objectives and goals of ordinary men? The answer was that while he sought to avoid the ordinary pursuits of career-minded men, he could no longer find satisfaction in his chosen avocation—his intellectual career. It seems that his affair in the corporation permanently shattered his intellectual tranquility. He could no longer read with a relaxed frame of mind. In Nietzche he saw the will to power that drove the members of his executive committee. In Sartre he saw the absurdity of all life, including his own. In Fromm he saw alienation of business executives in grotesque proportions. He could not read without distorting the meaning of his great men and intellectual saints, and he could not argue without recalling the unanticipated consequences of his presumed disloyalty. Oliver Dansby could not intellectualize the real world of ordinary men; he could not lose himself in the noble ideas of great men. Neither his intellectual nor work world was safe from the intrusive effects of the other. At least this was the case when he first came for counseling.

The case of Oliver Dansby is instructive because his self-centeredness was not related directly to conventional notions of authority and organization. In this sense, he was different from Sam Cory. Sam wanted to excel in the world of ordinary men. He wanted everything that the success drive afforded. Oliver Dansby wanted none of these things. He merely wanted to be left alone, to be free of the aims that propel men against each other. He wanted to be merely an innocent bystander to human events. In effect, his motto was, "Stop the world! I want to get off." His minimum involvement in the world of work was to provide the economic necessities of his intellectual life. He failed in both worlds.

The corporation was taken over by a president who got a huge increase in salary and proceeded to milk the corporation of its little remaining capital. Oliver Dansby could have spelled the difference between a corporation that survived and grew and a corporation that dissipated its strength through disorganization and madness. What the corporation needed at that time was someone who could take a firm position predicated on the organizational necessity for centralized authority. The controller was offered this unique opportunity partly because of the crucial nature of the facts and figures that represented the corporation's financial status. Oliver Dansby could not become involved in conventional matters of authority and organization. His notions of self were anchored in the great books and giant men. Although their ideas could have given him rare insights into the affairs of ordinary men, he could not apply them practically and enjoyed them for this reason. Now he must bring the two worlds together in a unified, meaningful whole. His sanity depends upon confronting the realities of life with the wisdom of the men of the past.

Why the Wrong Men Get to the Top

The ends of organized living are not served either by the insatiable drive for power of Sam Cory or by the sterile intellectual exercises of Oliver Dansby. Sam Cory refused to yield to ideas and causes bigger than himself. He saw himself as above authority and organizational imperatives. His case illustrates how notions of self must be tempered by the principles of authority and organization. On the other hand, Oliver Dansby bowed to the wisdom of great men of the past, which made the present world unexciting and unreal. Ironically, his intellectual world became a perpetual nightmare.

Oliver's case illustrates the tragedy that awaits men and corporations when executives do not become moderately self-involved in their responsibilities. He may appear to be a freak to the reader, but actually the last decade produced many executives with notions of self fulfilled largely in enterprises external to their corporations. Men were moved rapidly to fill jobs that were created by vigorous growth. Some were ill prepared for their responsibilities, e.g., Alvin Peck and Oscar Hanson. Others had their fondest dreams prematurely realized by swift upward mobility. If they had relatively mild success drives, they lost their zip and enthusiasm to continue improving themselves. One vice-president of a large automobile company said, "By forty I had acquired more money and status than my father ever dreamt of getting. To my brothers and sisters I was their hero. Coming from a poor home, I became drained of ambition. Because I had more money than I knew how to handle wisely, I found that building an investment program was exciting and challenging. Gradually I withdrew my mind from my job. I guess I shall be a vice-president or something the rest of my career, but I don't care. I'm having a ball with my investment program. I have learned that there is a lot more to life than being a hardworking corporation executive."

This automobile executive reflects a disinterested orientation toward work similar to that of Oliver Dansby. Both had turned their backs on the serious pursuit of an executive career. During the last decade, the author counseled frequently executives of this type. For various reasons, they gave up their places in the race and gladly turned their batons over to the next runners in the relay.

The last decade of stupendous growth drained or reinforced the success drives of men unpredictably. During this period of record change and progress, the size and complexity of the giant corporation had a telling effect upon executive behavior. Men emerged with talents for coordination and team work. A myriad of small face-to-face groups began to dot the corporate landscape. Committees became almost as numerous as executives. Oliver Dansby had the kind of personality that appealed to many superiors during this period. He was smooth, mannerly, reserved, and permissive. He was promoted by Mr. Kearns because he got along with people well. He was a perfect specimen of the good human relations man. He never rocked the boat, never poked his nose into another man's affairs, never threatened his superiors; and because he was basically lazy, he never grabbed the ball and ran away with it. Because he always got others involved, he was strong on committee and group decision-making. He had the appearance of what became known as the democratic type of manager.

Men of Oliver's appearance moved to the top in large numbers. In many cases, they replaced the autocrats like Mark Whiting and Will Fowler. They were at best team men and at worst gladhanders. However, not all had false exteriors like Oliver Dansby's. No doubt many had the character to back up their democratic manners. But some fabricated their styles to fit the growing search for team men. They disguised themselves to better climb the corporate ladder.

The search for the good human relations man was just developing when Oliver Dansby was given his first position under Mr. Kearns. This wave of managerial democracy swept him to the top. With his well-fitted disguise, his trait of irresponsibility went undetected. One might question why he and others who masqueraded were not always discovered. Let us first note that some men were very clever at concealing their true intentions and motives. They had to be or their opportunities inside the corporations (Oscar Hanson) or outside (Oliver Dansby) would have suffered. Autocrats practiced assiduously projecting democratic halos. Noninvolvers like Oliver Dansby and the automobile vice-president ingeniously acted out their roles of concerned and dedicated executives. Only the foolish showed their true colors.

The second reason why mistakes occurred in the selection of men for top positions was summarized by Mr. Kearns, who was a major casualty in Oliver Dansby's affair. Speaking as the president of another corporation, he said, "I think we made a mistake when we inferred from the good human relations man's behavior corre-

The Perils of the Selfish Self

sponding motives. He was a new type to business and industry at the time. I guess we assumed that men who got along with people had advantages for the corporation regardless of their motives. Business has always been result-oriented. We believed that behavior was more important than character. Besides, we were the product of our times. Isn't there a famous school of psychologists that do the same as we? I think they are called behaviorists and infer intentions and motives from animal and human behavior. We were doing no more or less. If you give a manager an objective, you let him find the means to achieve it. Then you measure him by how well he achieved the objective and not by his choice of means, unless, of course, they are immoral or illegal. Managing by objectives necessarily oriented me to behavior and blinded me to intentions and motives. I know now that I must not trust a man simply because of his performance. Look at the executive who succeeded me. He is milking the corporation! Who ever thought that he would turn out to be a scoundrel? His performance in the auto parts division seemed conventional and proper at the time. When he fell heir to programs of centralized authority, he unmercifully shoved men around, and now he rules a tight autocracy. Now I know that character is as important as performance, but how do I detect it? There are no good tests and clever men can fudge on them. I have decided to develop managers who are alert to the qualities that lie behind managerial facades. . . . We can start by slowing down promotion. In this last decade, business moved men to the top too fast. Some men never stayed long enough to have their performance evaluated. My successor was promoted to the presidency before they discovered that his subsidiary corporation was broke. Now he has the authority to nullify and void his own failures. Men should be given special assignments to purposefully draw out their true intentions and motives. We do this occasionally, but not enough at the top levels. Too much dignity is involved. But at the top is where one should test for character. . . . As Oliver Dansby's case shows, weak or bad men at the top can ruin a corporation by their sins of commission or omission. . . . I, for one, have learned a lot about human character and, perhaps, I could not have gained this insight from normal situations. However, I hate to think that the only time true character emerges or can be tested is in times of great crisis. It would be terrible to have to shake up the whole corporation and men's careers in order to make better inferences about character. Anyway, I don't want the good human relations man anymore. I'm almost prepared to go for the rank autocrat. Of course, his motives and intentions are not as praiseworthy, consequently they are not subject to faking. For this reason, he can be trusted. I know that sounds strange, but who in his right mind would scheme to be arbitrary, domineering, powerful, aloof, rigid, and occasionally downright mean. These qualities are not exactly in vogue, you know. Chances are that if you find a manager who behaves this way, he is acting true to character. Or is it possible that some would fake these qualities to get ahead? I think not. Anyway, I resolved that I would give the glad-hander a thorough going over the next time I got one close to me. I have one in my sights now."

Mr. Kearns was an eye witness to one of many typical scenes that emerged in the big business corporation during the last decade. Unfortunately, he still underestimates the capacity of human beings to be splendidly wicked. There is no assurance that ambitious executives will not fabricate autocratic styles to enhance mobility. In his present corporation, he has made abundantly clear his distaste for the good human relations man. Chances are that a few of his subordinates are rearranging their styles to accommodate his definition of a good executive. The reader may recall the cases of Sam Cory, Mark Whiting, and Oscar Hanson to see how executives will compromise to secure their aims of mobility.

Nevertheless, Mr. Kearns stated a growing conviction of many executives today. In many corporations the good human relations man is held suspect. However, the pure autocrat, like Mark Whiting or Will Fowler, is not proving to be the only alternative. We have seen evidence of the disadvantages of the two extremes. Authority, in order to be productive, must be sensitive to and modified by the objective ends of corporate organization and by the dignity and self-worth of the individual members. In turn, the notions of self held by each executive must be a product and process of organized enterprise and must be amenable to the influence of authority. We have seen in the cases of Hawley Simpson and Alvin Peck what happens to careers and corporations when notions of self and concepts of authority are mismatched and disparate. The cases of Oscar Hanson and Olaf Johnson illustrate career and corporate difficulties that ensue when notions of self are out of kilter with the objectives and needs of organization. The cases of Sam Cory and Oliver Dansby illustrate the tragic consequences that may occur when the self-identity becomes inflated above or detached from the crucial responsibilities of corporate management.

The successful executive does not elevate the principle of authority above the objectives and goals of his corporation. He does not view authority as an end in itself. To Alvin Peck, authority had such a powerful magic that to be near it was to feel secure and to hold it in his hands was to feel threatened. The successful executive believes that the goals and purposes he sets for this corporation are subject to validation by some authority set, be it his superiors, board of directors, or the various interest groups that levy claims upon the corporation. Will Fowler learned this lesson from his career crisis.

The successful executive's notions of self allow him to believe that his corporation is something that deserves his best talents. Sam Cory was a disbeliever, as was Oliver Dansby. For different reasons, they could not humble themselves before man-made institutions. Sam served his bushy ego and Oliver his estranged intellect. Whereas Sam continues his pathetic struggle for self-aggrandizement, Oliver Dansby appears to be making a gradual adjustment to his new situation. In time, he will probably regain his intellectual concentration but never his privacy. He no longer wants to be non-involved in the real world. He is preparing for graduate work in history and philosophy and hopes to become a professor. In this role, he seeks to find the missing bridges to the real world of work and life. He is active in civil rights programs, civil liberty causes, freedom of speech movements, and the far left campus organizations. Nearing the age of forty, Oliver Dansby wants to be helpful to young people who mistakenly seek in their academic studies escape from their personal assumption of responsibility and involvement. He believes academic people should be activists. If he has his way, few students and professors will be in their ivory towers. They will be in the street marching.

8

THE CRISIS OF THE LAST STEP

Failure follows swiftly on the heels of success. Occasionally it overtakes the executive and demolishes his way of life. The men in this book have experienced the failure of success even though they have achieved positions of honor and distinction. They are important figures in their communities and society, earn salaries that represent the five percentile of income, and are models of success to many people. But success has failed to give them quietude.

Inwardly they are incomplete men. Mark Whiting, chairman and executive officer of an educational consortium, secretary of the board of Universal Chemical Company, senior advisor, community and national figure, and friend of many, said in confidence to the author, "You know, I have almost made the adjustment. I know I won't be president. I can almost live with myself. Almost!" Will Fowler, former president of two companies, a father of three very fine children, a devout layman in his church and leader of many religious organizations, a man of independent wealth, said, "I would rather die than remain for the rest of my life the director of corporate planning and development for my corporation."

Success has failed to bring rest and repose because of the gradual distortion of the achievement drive. This drive has become geared to success at all costs. In the early- and middle-management phases, the upwardly striving manager dares not allow himself to set his goals on the presidency. He looks upward and to the center of the corporation. The object in focus is a small group of men who, with the president, run the corporation. It is almost as if the young manager is saying to himself, "If I set my goal for the presidency,

The Crisis of the Last Step

I may be sadly disappointed. I shall be happy to become a member of his executive group." The executive group becomes the best opportunity to realize his achievement drive. Because they may number from six to twenty, the chances are greater of moving to this station or level. The middle manager sets his sights and begins to work his way up the many steps of the corporate ladder. At some point he may decide to go all the way. The executive group is no longer a terminal point. He must become president some day.

It seems that this total commitment is a function of the frequency of interaction with the president. If this is true, it occurs upon or after entrance into the executive group. Once this commitment has been made and has been reinforced by a few successes, there is seemingly no turning back; the executive's whole self becomes engaged in the move for the presidency. If he makes it, his fondest notions of who he is and can become are affirmed. He becomes a big person in the eyes of others and particularly himself.

But suppose he does not make it. Suppose his career becomes arrested enough to greatly jeopardize his chance of ever making it. Then this commitment becomes hazardous and filled with terror. This is the story of Mark Whiting. The last step happened to be the biggest. It was the final act needed to complete his development as a person. Without this final step, he does not feel fully developed, his identity is only partial. To this day, Mark Whiting feels incomplete, only part of a man.

When career arrestment comes to an executive whose achievement drive is directly tied to the presidency, a career crisis follows. A career crisis is a crisis of self. It is a painful, humiliating, and degrading experience. Some men destroy themselves. Directly or indirectly they may decide to do away with this "half of a man" that they have become or they may decide to stay alive and ruin those who are responsible. Their clever skills and managerial brightness may be used to reduce the efficiency and profitability of the corporation. (We may note parenthetically that the emotional cost of having only one president for each corporation must be enormous. It is an expense that does not show on a profit and loss statement.)

Where does all of this misery start? Ours is a society that places a high value upon success. It hands out big identities, so to speak, to those who have gone all the way. Great wisdom and competence are ascribed, status and dignity are granted to presidents of our great institutions, including big business corporations. It is understandable that the achievement drive becomes eventually affixed to the presidency. At this point the individual enters a phase in his life that holds out the possibility of both triumph and terror. Mark Whiting has been terrorized. He has experienced a penetrating fright every bit as intense and real as that encountered under combat conditions.

From the outside he appears to have made his adjustment. Inwardly, he cries out for relief. Just one more step and he would no longer be in pain. He would be master of his corporation rather than a prisoner, a boss of bosses rather than an appendage to a board of directors. In that final step, Mark Whiting would complete his selfhood.

But it is precisely the final step up the corporate ladder that Mark Whiting can not take. He has no one to sponsor him for the presidency. Few men arrive at the top who are not trusted by someone up there. Trust emanates from confidence in an executive's managerial skill and personal dedication. Mark Whiting has lost both of these qualities. He is not dedicated to the corporation as something bigger than self and deserving of being treated as an end. He needs the corporation as a means to his own self-fulfillment. His managerial skills have been dulled through lack of exercise and opportunity.

Although Mark Whiting may have been lacking in dedication and managerial skill before his career crisis, the way he handled his catastrophe made his weaknesses terribly apparent to others who could nominate him for the presidency or support him in a major role. His problem is not simply the mistakes that caused the career crisis, but the mistakes that were made in the attempt to master the crisis of self. The crisis of the last step ensues from failure to master the career crisis.

The Committed Executive

We have seen that in the last step the executive expects to complete his self-development. For this last step to have such deep meaning, at least two qualities must exist. He must first experience failure of the type that threatens his taking this last step. Failure is largely a subjective state of mind. Essential to it is a feeling that binds the executive to the role of administration. Failure to take the last step will become threatening when the executive is emotionally committed to the task of becoming an increasingly effective administrator. In other words, the second factor sets in when this bond between his notions of self and administrative role becomes sealed. Then failure will be interpreted as threatening. When the bond is cemented, the executive commits his whole self to succeeding in the administrative role. He expects to realize in success his fondest dreams of self-worth and respect. For this executive, failure of a very small amount may induce deep-seated fears and anxieties.

The committed executive has a style of life that largely pivots around his administrative role. By life style we mean the way in which an individual copes with his many areas of life. Life areas involve those activities that are more or less valued. Values are structured in a series of centric circles, with those at the center comprehending and organizing the peripheral values. These central values organize and direct that person in all of his characteristic areas or human activity and determine the unique way he will handle his life problems. His life style will show certain essential, predictable qualities that distinguish him from all others.

Counseling business executives shows that success in the administrative role is a central, if not *the* central value around which pivots their whole life style. The attempt to succeed in business has wide-ranging effects upon their religious, educational, political, economic, familial, community, and sexual roles. What is needed to prove this shrinking of his whole style of life to matters largely career oriented is evidence that the executive becomes completely wrapped up in his career demands and goals. This evidence would show that over a protracted period of time administration occupies a major share of his life. It becomes, so to speak, his whole life. Scientific evidence is not yet sufficient to clearly affirm this point. However, counseling evidence suggests that for the vast majority of executives life and work become overlapping and synonymous. Literally speaking, his life's work is to succeed as an executive. As the success drive is reinforced by acts of high performance, the last step takes on compulsive proportions. The presidency becomes a position that will justify the warping and disfiguring of the life style.

However, when the presidency becomes beyond reach, the many sacrifices made in other areas of life lose their meaning and value. The executive is without self-justification. To redeem himself in his own eyes he pours vast amounts of emotional reserves into the career scene. He may contrive a strategy or intuitively feel his way toward a solution. Whatever he does, it is to master his career crisis. All other life areas become affected by his fears and anxieties of failure.

The Case of Jonathan Barr *

Jonathan Barr represents a committed type. We shall see by piecing together his responses to his diagnostic interview below just how central to his life style was his administrative role.

When asked about his future advancement with the company, Barr said:

I won't stay here long at the present level. I should be president of the company in about two years. I'll test them out on it and if I don't think I'll get it, I'll start to look around. I feel I could run any business better than it's being run now. I wouldn't hesitate to take over the presidency of General Motors tomorrow.

When asked how willing he had been to change geographical locations to get his current position, he said:

If I felt a move was the best thing, we moved. Sometimes my wife didn't know about it until the day before the move, but she never objected.

Barr had this to say about his fellow executives:

I lie awake nights thinking of ways in which the firm can get ahead overnight. It's easy as falling off a log—they're stupid guys, the ones I work with, and the leaders of competitive companies.

Asked if any of the men he works with were close friends, Barr replied:

Who has any good friends? Maybe one or two, but if I left the present company I'd find new ones and the old ones would be forgotten. So would I. Oh, sure, I have plenty of friends. I could call any bank president in St. Louis and you'd have dinner with him because of my friendship with him. But it doesn't mean anything. I learned a long time ago not to form close attachments. It's easier to fire the guy when you are moved ahead of him. I think that's very important. Yet I'm friendly. I make a point of never hurting anyone unnecessarily, but rather try to make any place better for my having been there.

About the relationship of his wife to his career, Barr had this to say:

I've read the magazine articles that say a man should marry the girl with more of everything than he has, that through her contact with other wives he can get ahead. I've proved that this is not necessarily true and should write an article of my own to show how. Instead of marrying up, I married down. My wife had less of everything, money and contacts, even, than I had. I've kept my home life completely separated from business always. My wife has never met my business associates' wives and never will if I can help it.

About his relationship with his wife, he said:

My wife just plain don't know what I've done. She'd be more interested in me being a $60-a-week grocery store clerk and be home. My wife is very adaptable, however. She works out things the way I want them to be. She doesn't interfere with my business life at all. She's very tolerant of my comings and goings. She had to adapt herself to my necessities.

Barr had this to say about his basic approach to people:

There was a principal at high school who taught me not to trust people, and some of the things in handling people I don't trust. I disliked him very much. He was very partial. He had the feeling that certain people in certain walks of life could help him get what he wanted. I said to myself, "You've got a fight on your hands that you don't fight with your fists." And I did it. That's what I mean by learning to be a man. If somebody does something to me, I'll take care of it if it takes fifty years.

Asked if he had any hobbies, Barr said:

Hobbies? I guess business is my hobby.

When asked about what he did on his vacations, Barr said:

Anywhere I go I'm pretty close to my business. There's always a tendency to connect the locality with your business. You can't drive through California without thinking this or that spot would be good for a branch. A long ocean voyage would be ideal because you couldn't establish a branch there.

Of course, there is a lot more to Barr's style of life than what has been provided by this brief sketch. However, note that Barr's style of life offers little opportunity for hobbies, relaxation, vacationing, and simple fun. He has evolved a manner of handling people, including friends, peers, superiors, subordinates, and women, that marks him from others. This is what a style does for the person. Every child has an emerging life style. By the early forties this life style has become established. This is not to say that it does not change after it has been well established. Rather, it does change gradually if the person changes his values and orientation toward his environment. Seldom does a life style change radically over a short period of time. The exception is when the individual undergoes a crisis of some kind. We shall see that Barr's life style changed as he attempted to resolve his career crisis.

Barr was passed over twice for the presidency of his corporation. The first time did not seem to be a vote against him as much as a vote for another man who had certain timely qualities and experiences. But the second time created a disastrous effect upon Barr. Word came roundabout to Barr that he was too ruthless and insincere. The fact was that Barr gave every moment of his waking mind to his corporation. Even on vacation he would think of what was best for the corporation. Barr was committed psychologically to bettering himself by bettering the corporation. Around this axis his whole life spinned. Nevertheless, he was not viewed in this light.

Barr was viewed as a good second man and could remain in that position for the rest of his career. He was used usually to do the emergency work: cut down operations or enlarge them upon short notice. He was used often as a hatchet man and troubleshooter. He was a man given to extremes and could be very useful during emergency periods. But he was not and could not be a first man.

It is hard to say exactly when Barr realized the awful implications of this fact. He realized gradually that his values were out of kilter with what the corporation liked to see in their top man. He recalled the day in which the chairman of the board called upon him in his private office ostensibly to ask a favor. The chairman mentioned that he thought that the new president would be a good leader and that the corporation needed a good team man in the front office. Having been passed over for the second time in four years and having an extremely autocratic managerial style, Barr retorted in an extremely lengthy and aggressive fashion. Because it was very much his way of managing, the chairman seemed to expect this strong rebuttal. At this point the chairman said, "Well, John, I know of your point of view and respect you for it. Of course, you understand that you will not be jeopardized by your calling a spade a spade. In fact, I have been meaning to talk to you about the corporation for some time. Let's get together next week for lunch and discuss some of the problems." Barr, with considerable show of anxiety, asked, "What problem would that be now? You have picked the new president and he and I don't get along. Is this the problem you want to discuss? If so, I can be quite specific about it right now. You have made a very poor selection and I hope you don't expect other members of the front office to change their lives to accomodate a poor selection." The chairman merely replied, "I can sympathize with you, but let's talk about it at lunch next Tuesday. Okay?"

Although this delay of discussion was not particularly appealing to Barr, he had to abide by his superior's request. For one solid week, Barr went over in his mind all the things he was going to say to the chairman. He never suspected that he would not be allowed to say much at the luncheon and that he would have very little to say in the corporation thereafter.

At lunch the following Tuesday, the chairman carefully placed himself firmly in the driver's seat by choosing his club for lunch, his mode of transportation, his time of arrival and departure. He made it clear that he had exactly one hour and a half for lunch, and during the first one-half hour he defended his reason for rushing away so soon. Finally, he passed this remark, "John, you have been with us fifteen years. You came to us at a very high level and have secured two promotions. As a vice-president of manufacturing you have been extremely useful. Now we want you to become vice-president for special problems. You will start your new assignment Monday morning. You will report to me for a while."

Barr could not believe what he was hearing. Vice-president of special problems, impossible! he said to himself. He asked for clarification and was not satisfied by the reply. Then he asked for an explanation and got what shook him to the core. The chairman said, "Well, I don't fully understand why you feel negative about this promotion. Your salary will be increased substantially and you will be exposed more to the board through my office. It is quite a responsible job. The corporation today has many problems that do not fit its organizational structure. They cut across divisions and lines of authority. You are good at special problems solving and we need you at this post." And then the boom fell. "You know, John, you will never be financially hurt here. Not everybody can be president. Some men are by their very nature second men. You are a damn good second man." After this remark, the chairman's words fell upon deaf ears. John Barr was too shocked to listen attentively. He failed to note much of what happened on the way back to the office. His life became a nightmare after this eventful luncheon.

Barr's career crisis threatened his whole style of life. He could see that he was living improperly in the eyes of his superior. Although he had become well adjusted to his life style, he decided to change it in order to appear more appealing to his superior. To this day he has not given up becoming president some day. The committed type tends to have this "stick-to-itiveness." In the space of approximately two years, John Barr has successfully negotiated a new life style. Anyone interviewing him at this time would have seen a man who was extending himself into the community and social life. He was treating women with deference, patience, and respect. His wife simply did not understand her husband any longer. He could turn on the charm and become once again her suitor, and did so frequently. He even started telling her his career problems. He took up the search for important roles and offices in all kinds of nonbusiness organizations. Jonathan Barr was running for office on a platform of "be kind to people and dedicated to humanity."

In this attempt to change his life style, he made a lethal mistake. He underestimated the importance of his new job as vice-president for special problems. He saw this job as created for the purpose of getting him out of the hair of the new president. As usual, it was not to be taken seriously. The assignment in the research and development division, the assignment in Brazil, the assignment of corporation planning, and others were not given his total, undivided attention.

His superiors saw a major difference that made him even less appealing and useful. They saw a once strong, domineering, aggressive, and somewhat ruthless individual, who worked every moment for the corporation, become suddenly unresponsive to corporate demands and responsibilities. If Barr could not be used as a special problems man, what could he be used for? He certainly did not fit into the new team given his negative attitude toward the new president.

Barr thought that he was being given a shelf upon which to relax for the rest of his career. He did not suspect that he was actually given a responsible position. It was simply a mistake of judgment. However, the effect upon his career and life style was catastrophic. Before his promotion, everyone knew of him as a frank, straightforward, autocratic, and terribly ambitious man. Now they did not know what to think. Their doubt caused him to be passed over a third time.

During the third year after his promotion, the corporation found itself in a bad situation. Among other things, the product mix was out of kilter with market demand. It seemed that the front office was allowing the product mix to be determined by the research and development staff rather than by the customer demands and buying patterns. It would take a strong man in the presidency to change the corporation's emphasis and priorities, and the new president was not such a man. The chairman and his board of directors decided that a John Barr type was needed, but not John Barr. The chairman said to the author, "I really didn't believe that Barr could run the corporation the way we wanted and still be himself. During the last several years he has softened and mellowed. Why, he is even kind to women! I don't see how he could shake the rafters of a corporation that needs shaking badly. I decided to go outside and find a pure, unadulterated autocrat and give him a three-year assignment, after which he could retire or stay in the corporation as a senior advisor. So we passed up Barr the third time."

The point to be taken from John Barr's career crisis is that the warping of his life style actually brought on a greater crisis than that created initially by his career crisis. John Barr is now in deep trouble with himself. Will he revert to his former life style or continue to live according to his new life style?

The committed executive is dedicated to a life that puts first the managing of business firms. When this commitment is as total as is Barr's, it can not be easily retracted. Sometimes it can be reinforced by means of happenstance. For example, the new president who was brought in from the outside and who was very much the autocrat, knew of John Barr and of his reputation before his sudden change of life and decided to ask him to become his executive vice-president. The purpose was to use him as a hatchet man once again. Barr accepted eagerly and reverted to his old life style. Of course, he is and probably always will be a second man. Nevertheless, he holds out hope to execute the last step to the presidential suite. Such lasting hope and ambition stems from his deep-seated commitment to total success in the administrative role.

The "Success in Any Role" Type

The executive's whole style of life will vibrate from failure at work when success at work becomes his whole life. The committed executive is dedicated to finding success in the managerial role. Counseling of executives shows a second type. He is the "success in any role" type. He has a relatively weak identification to the administrative role. He stands emotionally next to his managerial job but, unlike the committed type, is not firmly attached to it. The acid test is whether he can go home and freely and gladly leave behind those problems that beset him at work. The committed executive can not leave the hammer in the air when the whistle blows signalling the end of the work day. He takes his work home with him and into all areas of his life style. On the other hand, the "success in any role" type is an opportunist. He is more flexible in his life goals. If success does not come in one role, he may and must seek it in another. While the committed type has found a meaningful role whereby he hopes to establish and fulfill his identity, the opportunist is reaching for meaning in life and stands ready to get it where he can find it.

Let us look more closely at the profile of an associated type. Jim Walker's life style* evolves from an inactive concern for success in any one role.

When asked about his future advancement with the company, Walker said:

The Crisis of the Last Step

I have never asked for a promotion and I have never really aimed for one particular job. I do what has to be done and I always try to do my best. I never believed I would become a vice-president of this corporation and I don't know if I will become the president. I talk to the president often and he includes me in his difficult decisions. Hence, he has never given me reason to believe that I will be his successor. I will wait and see what happens.

When asked how willing he had been to change geographical locations to get his current job, Walker said:

We like to get deep roots in the community. Moving has always been a problem to my wife and I. My wife has had difficulty in the past in moving. I once turned down a big promotion with another company because she didn't want to give up our friends and our church, community and social relationships. I guess I would do the same thing again if my wife insisted upon not moving.

Walker had this to say about his fellow executives:

Most of my fellow executives are very competent managers. I look up to them and respect them. I make a practice of consulting them freely. The president is a truly great man. His mind works like a computer. I have taken over many of his decision-making techniques. The controller is a mathematical whiz. I am very fortunate to be a member of such a prestigious group. I lie awake nights counting my blessings.

Asked if any of the men he works with were close friends, Walker replied:

I have a few very strong attachments to my fellow executives. We play bridge every Friday with the president and his wife. The controller and I play golf together frequently and my assistant and I are luncheon partners. Of course, I have many acquaintances, probably too many. I don't feel as close to them as I do to my friends.

About the relationship of his wife to his career, Walker had this to say:

My wife is a very interesting person. Basically, she runs the home. She has her wide latitude in selecting furniture, food, guests, and friends. She largely determines the manner in which the children are raised. My wife comes from a well-to-do established family of New England. She is accustomed to having things a certain way that fits her family's traditions. I learned this when I married her and have adjusted to her patterns. I even joined her church. I think it is fortunate that she can manage as well as she does.

About his relationship with his wife, Walker said:

My wife is extremely involved in my career. I talk over everything with her. In a way she is very much like my president, sharp, clear thinking, and knows what she wants and how to get it.

Walker had this to say about his basic approach to people:

I like people in general. Of course, there are many of my friends and acquaintances who do not see things my way, but I get along with them very well. People have never been any problem. If you hurt them, they will hurt you. If you try to forget their errors, they will forget yours. I discovered years ago that I am less subject to criticism and hostility if I give way to the other person, especially when he is riding high and aggressive. Frankly, I have decided that people are not worth fighting over.

Asked if he had any hobbies, Walker said:

I have several hobbies. I collect stamps and coins and go four or five times a year to exhibitions or conventions. I also like to work with wood and have made some very fine cabinets and pieces of furniture. I rush home afternoons from work to lose myself in my hobbies. I really enjoy being by myself and away from the problems of people and congested organizations. I think every executive should have two or more hobbies. There would be less manipulating and fighting among my corporate staff.

When asked about what he did on his vacations, Walker replied:

I make a practice of taking my vacation every year. In addition, I try to steal away with my wife on business trips and usually have a few days to ourselves. I know that she does not enjoy leaving her friends during these brief periods of time, and sometimes I go by myself. Anyway, I like to be a man of the world and get out of my company and community to relax as often as possible.

Note that Walker's life style is radically different from that of Barr's. He has found room for vacation, friends, women, relaxation, hobbies. He is definitely not committed to becoming a great manager, and he is not terribly interested in having his managerial skill tested in the office of the presidency. When Walker goes home, he leaves his work at the office. He is and probably always will be a second man. He is crucial to the president because he is an effective buffer between his autocratic superior and managers below Walker

The Crisis of the Last Step

who seek a more human relations oriented boss. He is used as a buffer and enjoys the role.

He is not really a manager. He does not identify himself as a manager, does not like to risk, and fears making the tough decisions. But he does see himself as a successful person. He believes that he has achieved a lot in his family life, in his many hobbies, and in his community relationships. He is highly demanded as a member of boards and executive committees of trade associations, community and civic associations, and social organizations. He is a nationally prominent leader in his several hobbies. All of this makes for a man very proud of his many achievements, particularly those outside his work environment.

How, then, did Jim Walker react to his career crisis? As a second man and close friend of the president, Walker went the way of his president. When the corporation was ready to retire the president, they also made provision for Jim Walker to be moved to a less sensitive job and live out his career until retirement. When Walker was informed that he was being "kicked upstairs" to become secretary to the board, he happily accepted. He really felt relieved at the time. Until, that is, his wife heard about his career failure and until his many friends offered him sympathy and understanding. He realized that in the eyes of many he had failed and should be in a state of acute anxiety. But he felt that he had a new opportunity to work and enjoy people and life and actually looked forward to his new position. He determined that he would try as hard in his new job as he had in his old position. Although he could manage psychologically the negative definition that his friends ascribed to his "promotion," he could not handle the fears, regrets, and definition of failure of his wife.

His career crisis became centered upon his wife's ambitions and her concern about his career. He had definitely failed her and her family. She resolved that he needed to hustle more. The tranquility of his home and the excitement of his hobbies were shattered by the intrusive desires of his proud wife. He said, "She became unbearable. I guess she always was, but now she could not be handled. She climbed all over me morning and night. It got so that I could not go to the office without bringing my problems with me from home. At first I believed that she would adjust, but she actually got so bad that I delayed going home evenings. She became impossible to live with. So I did what any man would do. I shut her off by staying at work long hours and traveling a lot.

"You know how I got to be chairman of the board and the first man to get into this office without going through the presidency? I simply used the opportunities afforded me by the office of the secretary of the board to get around, make friends, know stockholders. And that last point is crucial. You know, stockholders have no effective voice in the company. They are always looking for someone to whom they can go for answers and information and support. I was that man. I found myself growing in stature and esteem in the eyes of some very important stockholders, some of whom were disgruntled and had no representation on the board. Really, Doc, it was like taking candy from a child. The new president was sitting on a powder keg about ready to go off, and all I had to do was just be there and talk to people. I found myself becoming their chairman.

"After one year in the secretary job, the chairman died of cancer of the liver. When the word got around to directors and stockholders that the chairman had a terminal illness, I found myself being invited to go to this and that meeting and even being asked to private homes of important stockholders for weekends.

"The chairman had not been dead a day before a very influential stockholder visited me to ask if I would accept the chairmanship. Well, I have never been one to turn down a job and said yes. I could see my wife smiling and happy for the first time in years. She would like this and so I offered to be their candidate. Well, to make a long story short, I was nominated and elected chairman of the board and had several representatives of the disgruntled stockholders placed on the board with me. I know that I did more than just wait for the opportunity, and I will work hard at this new job. But I don't place a great value upon it. It is not central to my life. In fact, I have not found any job in my career that really got into me (pointing to his chest). I guess I am not one of these guys who can find a job that really drives to the soul. Anyway, I have not found one yet."

It is apparent that Jim Walker is an associated type. He is not dedicated to the managerial role. He merely draws next to the role psychologically and can easily detach from it. But this is not the case of Jonathan Barr. He is glued permanently to the role of manager and hopes to find self-realization in it. To Walker, self-realization is becoming a well-rounded man with lots of achievements in areas of life outside the corporation. He is not completing his self-development by becoming chairman of the board. If anything, this new position will remove his annoying wife from the areas of life that he prizes highly, namely, his hobbies and home life. With her largely contented he is now able to continue to execute a style of life heavily dedicated to becoming a well-rounded individual.

The Committed and Associated Types Contrasted

The typical big business executive is emotionally committed to the task of becoming an increasingly effective administrator. This bond between self and the administrative role is often what people mean when they use the term "professional administrator." It so happens that the better part of administration has to do with matters of authority and organizational goal achievement. However, the counselor must see that these matters are relevant only insofar as they pertain to the administrative task. It is for this reason that a middle manager may have only fuzzy notions of the long-range goals of the corporation and still be emotionally identified with his managerial role. Being a good manager, he is no doubt identified with the subgoals of his section, department, or division, since these are within his administrative grasp. The same reasoning may be applied to authority and authority figures. In other words, while the middle manager may entertain distant emotional attachments with top authority and long-range corporate goals, his most intense attachments are with figures closer to his managerial task. At the top, of course, he attaches himself to top authority and overall corporate goals, since these symbols are close to his administrative task. Here his personal goals and the goals of the corporation become intimately fused.

An essential ingredient of an administrative career is the kind of attachment involved. In commitment, the individual may be observed to respond to the behavior of other people or objects by initiating in fantasy or in reality the same behavior in himself. Commitment tends to be subjectively identical. That is to say, the individual tends to behave as his interpretation of the other's behavior dictates and allows. It is possible to identify with objects as well as ideas. Administration is foremost a set of notions that an individual possesses about what he wishes to do and what is required of him in a particular occupational setting where matters of authority and organization are inextricably involved. He learns to identify with and become committed to these ideas by means of seeing how others assume the administrative role. He may distantly identify with superiors and goal-achieving activities, but he is essentially using these identifications to show himself how to achieve personal identification with the authority and goals of his own administrative role. This was evident in Jonathan Barr's case.

In the case of Jim Walker, the term "association" is more useful to designate the kind of attachment and may be used to convey the idea that an individual draws next to an idea or object but does not become firmly attached to it. Thus the middle manager or executive at the top may associate himself with his work role, but that may be as far as he goes. In a way, he practices disassociation (nonpsychoanalytic sense) because he has not the qualities and ambitions necessary to become firmly attached and absorbed by his work. Disassociation is relative and never complete. Even the worker feels at home to some extent in his role as an employee. However, many workers do not intensely identify with people at the factory or office. Their primary commitments are not with work groups, but self-selected groups at home and in the community. This is largely accounted for by the little opportunity to achieve personally and show tangible evidence of achievement in a highly organized, impersonalized mass-production factory. The worker associates with rather than commits himself to his work, corporation, and boss.

Some executives reveal, in clinical data, only weak commitment to the administrative task. This is not the majority pattern. Rather, the majority are emotionally anchored in administrative achievement. In a career crisis this may change, however, and the executive may become unduly concerned with particular aspects of administration. These possibilities are described in previous chapters under authority-, organization-, and self-centered patterns. This centering may occur as a response to acutely felt anxiety. The ideal would seem to be to identify with the administrative role as a balanced, integrated scheme of notions of authority, organization, and self.

How the Committed and Associated Handle Anxiety

The importance of acts of attachment lies in the effects upon the life style. Young men whose emerging styles fit them favorably for the lower managerial roles may find through identification a permanent way of life. They come to attach themselves to the managerial and, later, upper administrative roles so that their whole identity becomes directly affected, enriched, or restricted. By the time they are ready for the executive ranks, their careers occupy the greater share of their lives.

In numerous instances, the author has noted that executives who are committed to the administrative role may practice association with other roles in the community—school, political party, or charity organizations. They may drop these roles and take on others, largely because of how they relate to their administrative identification. Whereas they may be emotionally capable of dropping all of these activities in the other life areas, they cannot long endure the thought of not being an administrator. Clinical experience shows that perceived success and failure in the administrative role helps to predict the kinds of activities valued by the executive in outside organizations and how they will be approached. Often, the executive will interpret his administrative role to include participating in these outside affairs. These external activities may be associated with, not identified with. In such a case, the executive may become a director of a community campaign fund, not because he really believes in it, but because this is what a successful person can do and what a business executive should do. Because all other life areas become nucleated around the administrative role, the executive enjoys internal consistency and self-consistency. We may speculate that he is successful in the administrative role because all other life areas are committed to the primacy of administrative success.

In the case of acts of association (drawing next to but not

being firmly attached) the career does not enjoy the full support of the whole pattern of life. There may be intrapsychic compartmentalization and even conflict because of the hesitation of the individual to commit his whole life to the tests and strains of administration. Many times it is found that individuals who have an unconscious fear of failure actually contribute to their failure because of the disassociation of life style from the career.

When the whole living pattern is committed to the successful performance of administration, vast amounts of energy are made available that otherwise would be held back. The life style directs energy into activities which can be assimilated with it. When these activities are held alien, energies are withheld. Failure or precarious marginality may result.

The successful executive is typically a high energy type. He freely expands vast amounts of psychological and physical energy in the administrative task. Inwardly, he is not in conflict because through positive commitment with the administrative career, he enjoys the support of the life style. He has first things first and has organized his whole life accordingly. Because of the affinity between his total identity and his administrative self, blockage of the latter is recorded psychologically as blockage of the former. When his success as an administrator is threatened, his whole self-identity may become threatened.

This executive can no longer sit as comfortably on outside boards and committees owing to his perceived failure in his occupational area. Such a failure may create a career crisis threatening his whole life style. Thus a career crisis may become a crisis of the total self. Likewise, because of the affinity between administrative career and life style, knowledge of the former provides insight into the latter. The counselor can gain information about the whole person by knowledge of his administrative career. In association types, this is not possible and calls for a different handling of the case.

Administrative commitment is more or less an unconscious act. This is what differentiates it from administrative association, which is a more casual response to the immediate objective demands of the job. In administrative commitment, the client who comes for career counseling is not aware of how his whole life pivots around his administrative role. Identification with the administrative role actually involves the absorption of large quantities of the total self.

The threat of separation from the administrative role reveals anxieties that penetrate his whole concept of self. These gross anxieties may be denied their full implication. The client may deny that they mean so much to him as to make him uncomfortable at home, in church, in the community, and so forth. This act of repression may give rise to symptoms of behavioral disturbances in these other life areas. This is a form of displacement. It is not uncommon to find dysfunctioning in the client's parental, social, and community roles, or his role as husband. Through repression, separation anxiety may become generalized to the whole life areas. The complaints may or may not be about these disturbances in human relations in nonbusiness activities. Often complaints are limited to the administrative situation. Seldom does the client initially know how severely his whole life style is being threatened. He expresses a more or less subclinical difficulty having to do with a specific administrative problem about which he is gravely concerned. Further information may show how much he has staked his whole life on his administrative career.

It may frighten him when he is confronted with the full implication of his career crisis. Until then, he may maintain great faith that if worse comes to worst, he will not be fired. (At the executive level very few are actually fired. The failures are frequently put on nicely prepared shelves, often with additional pay.) Or he may feel that he can start over again, which, of course, is not possible because of his age. Few corporations that can afford his salary and need his competency will hire him at lower levels because pension rights, stock options, and ancillary privileges become far too expensive. He may feel that he can go to work for another company at his present level or higher, but this idea becomes threatening to him too. The reason is that he becomes fully conscious of how much his present administrative role means to him, and failure in it means failure in life. He must succeed in the present role because his whole life style presses toward final success. Anything less, such as a shelf or movement to another corporation, is a recognition of failure and becomes a source of intense threat. These thoughts are held alien to self, and unreserved attention is devoted to overcoming the immediate administrative difficulty.

The executive who forms an elementary association with the administrative role faces his crisis situation somewhat differently. Typically, he is motivated to perform well, not by the satisfaction of administrative achievement, but by the satisfaction of the secondary rewards of money, power, prestige, and status. These secondary rewards have become primary. When this is the case, separation from the immediate administrative situation may not be intolerable if those secondary rewards are not threatened. Shelving or lateral employment may be positively received. However, if these secondary rewards are threatened, he may tailspin just as acutely. In this case, his crisis situation may be extended to invade his whole life. His social, family, and religious life may evidence difficult human relationships.

It must be understood that his tailspin is qualitatively different from that of the committed type. With the latter, his crisis becomes generalized to the whole life style because the administrative style is threatened. He has identified with the administrative role and the primary rewards of achievement. In the former case, the client has identified with the secondary rewards of money, power, status, and prestige and made them the central values of his life style. He, too, cannot sit as comfortably on outside, nonbusiness boards and committees, not because he is a failure in his job, but because he so desperately wants the glory, status, and power that comes with his job. Of course, he may actually want to stay on these boards and committees because he genuinely believes in their purposes. In such a case, the above statements have no relevance. We all know, however, the individual who searches for the glory in the high-status job and in the high-status positions in the community. Of course, his career crisis may be felt every bit as intensely as the other, but its genesis is entirely different. It is quantitatively similar, qualitatively different.

Jonathan Barr and Jim Walker are two cases in point. Barr allowed the shrinking of his life style so as to become totally synonymous with his administrative career. Walker fought this desperately. He refused to allow the corporate ladder to be the sole or even major yardstick of his self-worth. His career crisis resulted from pressure from his wife to give more importance to mobility in the corporation. In contrast, Barr's career crisis stemmed from overcommitment to success in the corporation. In this sense, Jonathan Barr, Mark Whiting, and Will Fowler are similar. They are representative of the upwardly mobile executive whose commitment to the goals of success exceeds his capacity to achieve it. They are overcommitted in the sense that they lack the tools to sustain success and to absorb failure. They are vulnerable to the crisis of the last step.

9

THE NEUROCRATIC EXECUTIVE

An executive neurosis is precipitated by the acute stresses and strains of the administrative job. A neurosis may be defined as an unproductive solution to an intense problem. To be unproductive, the solution must not ease the basic problem. It may, however, yield certain side effects that are accepted as useful and advantageous in their own right. For this reason, the unproductive solution is applied endlessly, leaving the problem unresolved and the executive in a state of chronic anxiety.

It is popular to believe that a neurosis will lead to greater career failure. The logic behind this belief contends that the emergence of a career crisis brings about an unproductive solution that adds to the scope and threat of the executive's career crisis. However, this simple train of thought fails to account for the fact that neurotic solutions may dress up failure to look like success.

A neurotic executive may become administratively successful because he is neurotic. His neurosis holds certain advantages for his corporation. Such an executive may be classified as a neurocrat. (*Neuro* means emotions and *crat* means ruler.) While he is successful administratively, he is not successful personally. His neurosis is productive to his role, but unproductive in mastering his anxiety. The prescription for a would-be neurocrat is to become a chronically anxious executive who acquires a neurosis at the right spot at the right time.

The Inside and Outside Solutions

Before we observe the neurocrat more closely, let us review several crucial points. We have seen that a career crisis may overwhelm the executive so that he may comprehensively identify with his administrative role to the exclusion of all other areas of interest. Or he may rely totally upon outside interests and alienate himself from his administrative role. We will call the former the *inside solution* and the latter the *outside solution*.

The executive who feels incomplete because he has failed to place a steady foot on the last rung of the corporate ladder may find a solution outside of his corporation. He may attempt to complete himself through the agency of extra-organizational activity. Charity, religious, social, political, and governmental organizations may become the means of self-fulfillment. Into these roles he may thrust his whole self to the extent that he withdraws vast amounts of psychological and physical energy from his administrative role. By so doing, he may jeopardize his remaining chances for success in his corporation.

In this way, his attempt to master his career crisis may actually create a greater crisis. The additional prestige obtained from these outside roles may make his failure inside the corporation all the more ignominious. The crisis of the last step may tax his powers and skills and bring him to a breaking point. To avoid complete emotional failure, he may permanently sacrifice his executive position. He may simply quit his job, or he may simply discount his executive role and psychologically withdraw from his corporation. We have seen that men who have experienced the crisis of the last step have sacrificed many things that were dear to them in the hope of completing their notions of self-respect and self-worth. They have changed their whole patterns of life, in the hope that their newly created styles of life will bring permanent release from their feelings of incompleteness. Will Fowler is a case in point.

If either the *inside* or *outside* solution is the only one taken, the executive may not be classified as neurotic. This solution must be unproductively applied or be unproductive in essence. In the latter case, its unproductive essence represents a level of immaturity that becomes blindly used and relied upon as a desperation measure. Suppose a superior in the corporation saw usefulness in him. In other words, suppose his inside or outside solution appealed to the corporation at the time that it was being executed. A promotion at this time could make him organizationally productive. However, he may still feel vulnerable to a career crisis and overwork the unproductive solution. Hence, he would be classified as neurocratic.

The question is, Why does the executive adopt an inside or outside pattern in an attempt to resolve his career crisis? The answer is that the terrifying blow of a career crisis causes the executive to concentrate totally upon his threatened self. In the use of the inside solution, energy is drawn from social, community, family, and recreational activities to be focused intensely upon his career in the corporation. In the case of the outside solution, energy is drawn from his job and invested heavily in his family, community, social, recreation activities. In both cases, energy is concentrated upon defending the threatened self.

A man who adopts the inside pattern displays an inability to concentrate on outside activities. The stresses and strains of a career crisis eat away at his reservoir of energy. He feels compelled to take the dwindling energy he has available and bring it to bear upon his work in the corporation. But his energy is not spent in the corporation solely. Because his career crisis weighs heavily upon his mind, it occupies his thoughts even when he is with his family and social groups. The inside executive devotes his whole waking day to his career crisis, regardless of where he may be at any given time.

The symptoms of an executive following the outside pattern may be less apparent. The blow to the executive is so deeply disturbing to him that he may turn his back on the corporation and those who have dealt him this lethal blow. He rationalizes that a career filled with terror of this kind is not worthy of his continued efforts. He seeks meaningful activity elsewhere. Hence, the outside solution may be displayed by an executive regardless of the context in which he finds himself at any given time, including the office situation. While at work he withholds energy to be later used in his home or community.

The Defenses of a Neurotic Executive

When the executive fails to master a career crisis of catastrophic proportions, the crisis grows larger as he begins to feel inadequate. If mastery is delayed long enough, he may come to acknowledge the presence of superior powers over which he has no control and seek desperately for some means of controlling them. Thus he may resort to methods of defense similar to those used by a child who has not lived up to parental expectation.

The child interprets everything as reward or punishment meted out by higher powers. In a similar fashion, the executive who regresses to childlike logic may come to feel reproached, punished, and abandoned for having failed to support and pacify the great figures of his corporate family. He may take refuge in the defenses of a child who cowers before his angry parents. In this posture he may defend himself by acknowledging that he is wrong, incompetent, disobedient, and deserving of being the prime target of corporate wrath. By this means he bows to his superior's capacity to forgive and to restore him to the bonds of fraternal and corporate life. His defense mechanism is effacement.

Another defensive measure is the appeal to aggression, in which case the executive may revert to childlike instincts of blind fight. He may counter-target his superior and the corporation and resolve that if he survives their onslaught, he will destroy them with whatever forces he can muster from within himself, his corporation, and, if need be, his society. His technique is to stay alive to some day become the attacker.

The executive may also appeal to the child's defensive technique of resignation. In this case he may simply flee from his crisis situation, either physically or psychologically, or both. If he successfully executes a withdrawal maneuver, he may feel an intense fear and dislike for any human situation that even vaguely resembles his career crisis. For that matter, once the executive has been a target of a lethal corporate attack, he has a built-in aversion for any kindred danger or threat.

The neurotic executive may appeal to one or to all of these defenses in the attempt to relieve his anxiety. In short, administrative anxiety of the neurotic kind may develop strong identification with outside life that tends to minimize the mundane requirements of administration, or it may develop strong identification with the administrative role that tends to minimize and reject other values and areas of life. All three techniques represent regressions back to attributes of previous life styles, usually associated with adolescence and preadolescence. In such regressions, previously inflated notions of self break through in the form of idealized or unrealistic images of self. In the inside solution, the inflated self is manifested in the using of the instruments of authority and the setting of organizational goals and policies with little regard for reality and the shared opinions of others in the corporation. At times it is more than the individual can do to be civil to other members of the executive group. Reality-centered tasks in the corporate system, such as reports, committee deliberations, or scientific studies may be relegated to the wastebasket of imperfection. He alone wishes to decide, can decide, must decide. The corporation is placed in jeopardy by the nincompoops in staff and by the technical psychoses of production people. If he is in production, the marketing people appear as grave threats to the corporation. In actuality, all may become puny in his eyes.

In the outside solution, the idealized self shows up in the utter disregard for business authority and goal-setting activities. These become unclean, crass, materialistic, selfish, inhuman, or socially irresponsible. He turns to the noble life areas outside the corporation and seeks a haven by identifying with society. Profitability, return on capital investments, liquidity, or even statesmanship appears to the idealized self as beneath dignity and self-respect. It is not that these activities and the people who perform them are puny (shame anxiety) as in the inside solution. Rather, they become grossly immoral. His idealized self incurs feelings of sin, which are projected onto others. In the outside solution in which the idealized self incurs neurotic guilt, the executive feels guilty for having spent the better part of his life in immoral, materialistic servitude. He feels punitive toward all other business executives, either for their ignorance of the real facts of life or for not facing up to them.

In either case, the executive seldom withdraws physically. Typically, his mission becomes one of vindictiveness and he cannot accomplish it by bearing this guilt or shame alone. They should feel guilty or ashamed, and he will help them feel guilty or ashamed. He sets his course of administrative action to achieve his ultimate vindication and their ultimate defeat. These inner dictates cry for proof and support. He compulsively works his solutions, varying only their behavioral attributes. These latter he sets forth with sometimes the flair of an actor playing several parts in the same drama.

Neurotic Aggression

The *aggressive* technique manifests itself in movement against authority or goal-setting activities, or both. Left far behind is the challenge of achievement—of having an exciting time at a given administrative task and looking forward to advances. In the inside solution aggression may show up in attempted seizure of power and authority. The individual may so wish to earn his authority that he will use fair means or foul. Ultimately he seeks total domination. In goal- and policy-setting activities he may be just as aggressive, using the goals and policies of his own department to thwart those of other departments. He may take logical, well-thought-out positions that show the importance of his department. He may work his group hard to show proof of his superior capacity to set high goals and organize for their achievement. The efficiency and superiority of his department may be realized at the expense of the corporate welfare. Nothing matters but that he shame others whose puny statures deserve his condescension. This technique was used by Mark Whiting.

The outside solution uses the aggressive technique by rebelling against life in the complex, massive corporation. This shows up in the individual's carelessness of his own authority and that of his subordinates in making logical but unnecessary claims on the boss or on the authority set in general. He may rebel against hs own departmental goals and those of the corporation. He may twist them, turn them, and reshape them to reduce the sting of immobility. He may plead for such social or human values (as opposed to economic or business ones) as more social responsibility over profitability, or more stability and permanence rather than growth and opportunism. He may work hard to show his colleagues the wisdom of "public utility" pricing and letting competition live. He may practice fair rather than free competition. Oftentimes he pushes his subordinates to identify with worthy, moral activities in the community. He is first and foremost an extra-organization man. The life outside beckons him, and he may make sure it beckons others in the corporation. He uses his authority to get his subordinates to participate in community affairs. This appeal to life often calls him to turn to religious, charitable, and liberal ideologies. He may become a Sunday school teacher, a friend of the library, or a grateful and charitable alumnus. Life outside becomes neurotically embraced through corporate and personal activities and goals. This technique was used by Oliver Dansby.

Neurotic Effacement

The techniques of *effacement* essentially involve moving with or into, rather than against. Here the appeal is to love rather than hate and usually involves rejection of the individual's evolved administrative style. His administrative style is contorted to plead covertly for acceptance and affection from others. He shrinks himself in presence and competency. Anything suggesting superiority or triumph must be avoided. The anxious shunning of pride, triumph, or superiority is revealed in many ways. Privileges turn into liabilities, power differentials into communication bottlenecks, and legitimate requests into taking advantage of friendship. He fears triumph in goal-setting activities and, thus, sets very modest ones for his department and encourages the same for the corporation. He appeals to a more relaxed corporate setting and shows instantaneous affection for those who become ill or maimed in the horrible corporate struggle.

In the attempt to be self-minimizing, he slowly forgets what he knows, what he has accomplished, and what good he has done. He is quick, however, in seeing these qualities in others and offering them incessant eulogies. He foregoes the enjoyment of many pleasures normal for his high position because to enjoy them would be selfish. He seeks to exert little authority, relying mostly upon people's affection and respect to get the job done. All of these things are contrived for the gaining of attention, affection, sympathy, and love. His salvation lies in others. Through them he makes the administrative role bearable. They will give him peace and unity and the means to become the greatest administrator of them all—his own idealized self. His whole life becomes anchored around this administrative style. All others in his life areas become instruments of his idealized self. They are praised, adorned, and elevated to high positions. Members of the educational, religious, and charitable elites are openly eulogized and praised. Their achievements are blessed by little notes and letters personally addressed. Never an opportunity goes by to show what a wonderful boss he is. But these others are actually being used. He is showering them with plaudits because they really mean nothing personally to him. Actually, they are being sacrificed on the altar of business. He absorbs them into his administrative self by proving to them that he is a socially responsible and sensitive business executive. To prove his point and also to effect absorption of his whole life and administrative style, he carries to them the gospel of administrative love. He may practice on boards of education, in church councils, and in civic groups the philosophy of administrative love. This may involve specific examples of how business does practice administrative love and how they must not fail to benefit from this great technique. His administrative style creeps into all areas of his life. In the life areas he practices association, not commitment.

The appeal to love may be found also in the outside solution. Here the executive rejects his evolved identity acquired from his administrative role. He struggles to achieve attention and affection principally from the world outside business. This means that he transports little of business life, its successes and values, into his other life areas. Instead he seeks ways of gaining love, sympathy, and affection by making his primary contacts in church, civic, charitable, and educational affairs. He identifies with these outside organizations. The values basic to the external institutions are eventually carried into the corporation by his socially responsible stride. The business firm may become an educational institution with emphasis on training for all, or it may take on the appearance of a religious institution in which individuals become reattached to the brotherhood of man through love and sympathy. Vast amounts of money may be appropriated to help colleges, widows, and disabled employees. The union may be cheated out of the privilege of bargaining because he is always one step ahead of them in representing the employee's welfare. Labor costs may rise, profits shrink, and liquidity be cancelled out by corporate welfarism. The corporation may eventually act like a charitable, educational, and religious institution all mixed together. Lost in the attempt to accede to the higher values of life is the narrow, efficient, profit-oriented administrative style of the past. It has become blotted out completely. In the process of showing love and affection for external groups, he has been diminished in stature. This, of course, is really what he wants. He wants to be lovable, and the more he appeals to others, the more he feels meek and small.

The moving against and the moving with patterns may evoke pseudo-autocratic and pseudo-democratic styles respectively. Few executives can be arranged into any one of these two styles completely. Each is a multicrat, adopting a unique mixture of the two. The reason for this amalgam is certain administrative deficiencies in the two patterns. Too much authority brings disadvantages as great as the disadvantages of too much democracy. Few pure types exist today because of the reality of the superior effectiveness of the multicrat. The neurotic executive clings to one type almost exclusively. He overworks it to the detriment of his administrative responsibility. He does not become an autocrat or democrat out of choice, but rather out of the dictates of his inner conflicts. He must adopt administrative extremes because he seeks a comprehensive solution. He hates compulsively or compulsively seeks love.

Neurotic Resignation

The third technique to resolve the conflict is found in a moving-away technique. It is basically marked by apathy and indifference, leading to psychological *resignation*. Here the executive achieves a pattern of withholding investment of energy. In the inside solution, energy inhibition may occur in his work pattern. Other areas of his life at first may appear unaffected. In the adminstrative situation there is a noticeable lack of goal-directed activity and thinking. The goals of the firm lose their challenge; the corporation ceases to be a meaningful object. He basically becomes an onlooker, peering at people as though they were completely strange, detached from him. Restriction of wishes, inaccessibility to others, and depersonalization of the administrative scene may develop. He becomes super-sensitive to pressure, orders, schedules, changes, and involvements of any kind. At best, he becomes a well-adapted automaton; at worst, a cantankerous old man. Seeing no special gifts in his superiors, he becomes intractable to them. He cannot be moved by airs of prestige, indignation of superiors, or rivalry of colleagues. He slips into oblivion, with one hand remaining in the life areas external to the firm. Here he is still at home, but perhaps not for long. The administrative career may eventually take over all of life. He may appeal to resignation in all his social, community, and family relationships.

In the outside solution, energy is not inhibited primarily in the administrative area. The executive may become resigned to the dictates of family life, give in to his children's wishes, completely submit to "momism." He becomes inaccessible to old friends, drops engagements of long standing, forgets and then purposely drops out of poker, bridge, or other kinds of social enterprises. He comes home each evening to sit and do very little. Television consumes him until he falls asleep to be rudely awakened in the wee hours of the night by the termination of broadcasting. His wife becomes sloppy, her age shows, her attractiveness is gone. He resists her suggestions, helpfulness, or submissiveness. Although he reserves himself each night for the battle of the next day, this battle, too, may lose its challenge. His whole life style becomes dominated by the resignation of his administrative career.

To the reader, the mechanism of resignation, activiated initially in areas outside the administrative role, may seem to be unrelated to administrative anxiety. Therapists are familiar with life problems that seemingly have no bearing upon occupational successes and failures, and many, of course, do not. In such cases, the anxiety or neurotic disturbance is not anchored in the administrative role and cannot be classified as administrative anxiety or neurosis. But it is well known that anxiety may be initially displaced upon innocent objects. This is entirely possible for administrative anxiety. In such a case, disturbances may first appear in areas seemingly alien to business administration. Some executives are so closely tied to the successful performance of the executive role that anxiety in that role will not be allowed. Because acute anxiety may not always be successfully repressed or denied, it may pop up in alien contexts.

Of course, an executive may incur a great disappointment in a nonbusiness role with which he has intensely identified. This anxiety may spill over to affect his administrative performance. This is what is meant when personnel men say, "You can't hire a pair of hands, the whole self comes to work." But does it always? Some persons have sufficient ego strength to compartmentalize the emotions or to work creatively to alleviate them in the contexts of their origin. Under these circumstances, they may not bring nonbusiness-anchored anxieties into their administrative role performance. Likewise, some executives who incur administrative-anchored anxiety may not displace its effects upon outside innocent activities and objects. This control of anxiety formation appears common to many successful executives. If administrative success is intensely sought after and blockage to this dominant drive occurs, and if the self is not strong enough to handle the anxiety, anxiety may be either displaced onto innocent objects and alien life areas, or focused on the basic causes or both. Mild anxiety may be restricted to specific objects or situations, and acute anxiety may pervade the whole life style. We turn to examples of neuroses of this latter kind.

Norman the Neurocrat *

When held in bounds by the reality of corporation life, neurotic solutions may be an asset. When a neurotic element is attached to cooperation, considerable gain may come from the ensuing teamwork and high morale. When excessive aggressiveness is diminished by a mild case of neurotic indifference and resignation, advantages in the form of stability and consideration may be expected. Not all fail who evolve neurotic components in their administrative styles. In fact, many seem to succeed, and through their successes keep down the neurotic element. They literally work themselves back to more tolerable levels of anxiety and away from the dangerous psychoses. In short, the neurocrat is often successful because of situationally acceptable amounts of aggression, effacement, or resignation.

Today, men at the top of the big business corporation show an active concern for problems of society that lie outside of the immediate administrative role. The executives of oligopolistic concerns have the necessary absence of traditional restraints to theoretically project the corporation into a socially responsible orbit. Clinical experience with executives shows that sometimes this identification with society comes from neurotic solutions to administrative anxiety. This act of statesmanship lacks the quality of sincerity. It stems more from the attempt to allay intrapsychic conflict than from a genuinely enlarged view of corporate citizenship.

It has been seen that the individual who pursues the executive career constantly grapples with problems of authority and organization. His notions of self are contained by these basic parameters, and idealized notions of self are somewhat inhibited by superiors who demand obedience and by organizational goals that require teamwork. But who or what constrains the executive's self-identity when he reaches the top? Imagine, for a moment, what dreadful fears and anxieties combat-weary executives may feel when finally at the top they find themselves free of dominating superiors and prescribed, limited organizational goals and policies. At the top, the administration function is today highly ambiguous. The classical forces of the marketplace, the liquidity and profitability requirements of capital-lending formations, and the restrictions of small ownership groups have been largely transcended by the nature of the large, complex business corporation. The top executive has more choices open to him for the establishment of corporate goals, and more choices open to him for the utilization of his authority and power. This ambiguity may attract neurocrats and may also help to produce them.

The case of Norman, vice-president of a huge corporation, is illustrative. His anxiety in the administrative role gradually grew into a neurotic need for effacement. Over the years, Norman had acquired an attitude very much like Theodore K. Quinn. As executive vice-president and next in line for the presidency of General Electric, Quinn suddenly quit because he could not see that a life devoted to making a big corporation bigger was worthwhile. In like manner, Norman grew to despise his administrative role.

It was as though he had suddenly seen through appearances

to the naked reality of corporate inhumanity, materialism, and indignity. Norman reacted with intense hate for the kind of administrative style he had perfected, and unconsciously projected this hate onto his corporation colleagues and business associates. He acquired idealized notions of self that exerted moral claims upon himself and others. He sought dignity in other life areas. He took on a vigorous program of community and civic responsibility. For this he received so much personal publicity and praise that the public image of the corporation was considerably enhanced. Because about this time the corporation was ready to move into a more statesmanship-like posture, he was promoted to the presidency. Norman accepted this promotion with ambivalence. He wanted to live a life different from that of a typical business executive. He saw this promotion as an opportunity to show that as a businessman he was a moral person. Yet he wanted to quit business life and get into a "human-centered" occupation. However, Norman was fifty years old and he could not turn around and start over. He felt that he must make the best of a bad situation. He pledged to be the kind of business executive that represented his ideal self.

Norman's corporation is a major oligopolist with considerable freedom from the restraints of classical business enterprise. Within three years, Norman has successfully spun off a foundation to aid scientific research and the education of scientists, got practically all men from division managerial levels and up actively engaged in a wide assortment of social responsibilities, written two books on statesmanship, given slightly more than two hundred speeches, and established a conference of businessmen and clergy for the study of business ethics and morals. For all practical purposes, Norman is a corporate philanthropist whose money is not his own but that of his stockholders. He has won a highly sought award, conferred upon him by a high governmental dignitary.

Norman is now searching for new ways to show his statesmanship, but often becomes deeply depressed because he has spent so much of his life in the role of business executive. These depressions are usually followed by intense efforts to articulate still higher meanings of social responsibility. Each time, these new thrusts psychologically shut off the disturbing elements in his prior and present administrative tasks. He is now chairman of the board and a prominent national figure, championing the social responsibility of the modern business corporation to provide humanity with the necessary weapons to fight poverty, war, and disease.

The tragic element in all of Norman's obsessive concern for mankind is that his idealized image of himself as a kind of "savior" has become for him a reality. He drives himself to actualize his idealized image without regard for the conditions of feasibility and his own psychic condition. Nothing is or should be impossible to him. On the other hand, everything is wrong with the world, particularly traditional, profit oriented business. His perfected, idealized image and the evils of the business world only make for greater inner conflict. Coerced from within, he flays randomly at the evils from without. His friends and many supporters are of the ultraliberal viewpoint and believe that the nemesis of modern civilization is irresponsible business gigantism.

Meanwhile, under his absentee administration, the corporation has become flabby, inefficient, and uncreative. Such dysfunctioning is made possible by oligopolistic practices of administrative pricing, live and let competitors live, and carefully contained and unilaterally dominated stockholder's meetings. We repeat, he practices safe enterprise, not free enterprise. Without this power of the corporation to be relatively indifferent to the forces of the market's price mechanism, Norman could not have so vigorously devoted himself to these activities external to the corporation. We may speculate that if more competitive forces were dominant in the industry, Norman would have had to be a working president and a chairman of the board more directly concerned with economic goals. Instead, he is now an international figure, periodically circling the globe, preaching the gospel of business morality.

To many, he is the epitome of business statesmanship. But to his counselor and confidant, he is estranged from what he actually is. Because he cannot live up to his implacable, idealized self and because he hates his real self, he is at war within. Behind his preachments of world peace through economic prosperity and moral responsibility, there lies an intense war against both idealized and real selves. It has been noted in human affairs that good often comes from evil. Norman's case may not illustrate this observation, however, because his appeals to statesmanship lack the moral seriousness of genuine ideals and regard for their feasibility and the conditions under which these ideals could be fulfilled. Norman's case may be illustrative of that "good" that dies with the man and never leaves behind a lasting monument to change and progress.

Neal the Neurocrat *

The case of Norman does not involve only the appeal to self-effacement. He is not simply trying to become an object of appreciation, love, and virtue. We have seen in his case description vast amounts of aggression indirectly unleashed against the people and the corporation symbolizing his hated administrative identity. The case of Neal is more uniformly illustrative of this neurotic appeal to aggression. Neal is the vice-president in charge of finance of a firm every bit as big as Norman's. He was formally trained in business administration and specialized in accounting and finance. Unlike many of the types who move around, in and out of the several functional areas before arriving at the near top to specialize in one administrative area, Neal moved to the top, staying in accounting and financial administration. By the time he reached the upper middle-management levels, it was too late to turn back or to move over to another function such as production, personnel, marketing, or research. His reputation had been firmly made in accounting and financial administration. However, Neal actively set his sights on becoming a member of the executive group and did not feel too disturbed by this institutional block to his ascending to the presidency.

When he arrived in the executive group as controller, he realized that he was not really a member of the "club." His opinion was asked for strictly in matters of finance, and then he was not allowed the full privilege of throwing his weight toward or against new corporate goals and their strategies. He felt *of* the executive group, not really *in* it. His marginal membership was a substantial blow to his self-esteem and dignity. He thought that matters of finance were crucial to corporate success or failure, and a representative of his competency should be vitally involved in administrative responsibility. As he moved around the periphery of the executive group, his repressed desire to become president emerged. This urge transcended all other values. He realized finally what his administrative career really meant to him. It all added up to the presidency, and there was no substitute for this achievement. He vowed that he would not be further humiliated. He was too good a man to be treated so ignominiously. He had come a long way, and no one, "not any one on this green earth," was going to cheat him of what was due him. "Besides," he said, "few people really know the company as well as I do." His growing idealized notions of self reduced to puniness those around him. He began to organize his resources to serve this implacable aim, shutting down emotional investment in other life areas. At home he became a man obsessed with the idea of becoming president. Activities such as family vacations and recreation lost their significance. Everything became subordinate to his career aim.

He learned that one's administrative ability was reflected in the size of the budget one was charged with directing. Since marketing and production were the largest, and finance and personnel the smallest, he conspired to show evidence of his administrative ability by increasing the size of the financial budget. This scheme took two directions. He set up a program to develop a computerized approach to accounting and financial activities and to help sell such an approach to marketing and production. He asked for and received training from a computer producer that gave to him a monopoly of knowledge and skills within the corporation. His program became successful enough to require more expert help. As this department of computer analysis grew, it reached out to help marketing and production. Soon his team of computer experts were informally directing many computer strategies and techniques in the departments of marketing, production, and eventually, research and personnel.

Because he studiously acquired and maintained this monopoly of expertise, a corporate reorganization plan placed him in charge of a new department, administrative analysis and control. Here he had access that few other executives had to information that virtually affected appraisal and evaluation of all corporate activities and goal achievements. Now he was a force to be reckoned with. The executive group, resistant at first, gradually acquiesced to his ascendency. Two members held out to fight against his leadership. He became executive vice-president of the corporation, a position especially created in the new plan of organization. Here his aggression took on clear-cut proportions. He began moving members of the executive group around into less threatening and crucial positions. He caused the premature retirement of one executive who had been a powerful figure in the past. He exposed another powerful figure as basically incompetent in this new technical world of the computer. He moved against people and ideas of the "old school" with a vengeance that was made possible only by his neurotic need for power and vindication. He did this at a time when the corporation was entering a rather shaky market picture and cutbacks in overhead were necessary. He moved against many employees in the lower-management ranks, causing over two hundred to leave. However, the president, chairman of the board, and other members of the inside board were extremely pleased with the positive financial picture that emerged.

Three years after he had set out to become president at all costs, he was formally elevated to this post by a grateful board. In this position, he proceeded to remake the whole corporation to fit his neurotic need for power and authority. Financial men who had served him loyally began appearing in substantial numbers in top executive positions in production, marketing, and even personnel. This acute change in mobility channels to the top caused vast numbers of middle managers to feel frustration and anxiety. He exploited these anxieties by rewarding those who were scared enough to defer to him completely. Now he had many members either actively dependent upon him or withdrawing their identification with the corporation to a minimum extent. Although neurotic, Neal had enough alertness to pick subordinates who had both abundant deference and sufficient competency. Six years after becoming president, he retired to become chairman of the board, leaving a handpicked successor, a toady in both appearance and manner.

Today there are many who speak of Neal as ruthless, heartless, authoritarian; at best, amoral and at worst, immoral. But few will deny that he gave the corporation what it needed, a complete shakedown. He is today a nationally prominent business executive who enjoys a fantastic reputation as an administrator. In his few speeches, there is little of Norman's social responsibility and corporate statesmanship. He believes in classical notions of competition—the survival of the fittest, the law of letting the devil take the hindmost. He is aggressively against government, liberalism, socialized medicine, civil rights, and human and political equality. He does little work in any of the life areas surrounding his business career. He helps with no civic, political, social, or charitable organization. He associates with his family, club, church, and "friends." He has no hobbies, disrespects his son's judgment and occupation (social worker), lives with his wife as though she were valued only for her instrumental qualities of making a home, preparing food, and being an occasional companion to prominent affairs.

One does not have to be his counselor to understand the intensity of his intrapsychic conflict. He overindulges in food, liquor, and cigarettes. He has frequent attacks of constipation. He came to the administrative counselor because a vice-president was acting strangely and was in need of career counseling. During this session he monopolized the situation with his Nietzschean philosophy of ruthless administration. It did not take much professional expertise to uncover the scheming that gave rise to his ascendency and success. He was very proud of his successful pattern of self-vindication.

Mr. Inside and Mr. Outside Compared

Neal's neurosis actively aided the success which others have attributed to his administration. Not all neurocrats become as successful as Norman and Neal. Many have unspectacular careers. The executive's neurosis must be highly attuned to the situational possibilities in order to actually contribute to administrative success. In fact, his neurosis often exploits an emerging situation, as the cases of Norman and Neal illustrate. In this sense there may be a relationship between a successful neurosis and situational realism. When the executive's neurosis is out of phase with the requirements of administrative success, or when the administrative situation is not auspicious for neurotic behavior, an executive may be cheated of a spectacular career.

What all of this suggests is that while the executive may be administratively free from the confining restrictions of the market's price mechanism, capital-lending institutions, active profit-minded ownership groups, he may not be free to make choices that stem from realistic notions of self. If autonomy means the capacity to order and make choices freely, based upon the principle of reality, Norman and Neal are not autonomous types. Each has actively contrived a style of administration and life that is born of intense feelings of weakness and unworthiness. Norman came to despise his administrative self and turned to active involvement in the life areas and values outside the firm. Neal came to despise all life areas except administration. Into this one category he threw his whole self. He fused business authority and organization into a symbol of power and put all of his resources into the struggle to become that symbol. Norman rejected the traditional power of business authority and organization as immoral and attempted to find justification and salvation in the moral haven of statesmanship. Into this category he, too, threw his whole self.

Norman illustrates the neurotic drive for love that identifies some, but certainly not all, executives; Neal, the neurotic drive for power. Eventually, all phases of their life styles were affected by the anxiety cued off by impending dangers to their evolving self-identities. Norman chose the outside solution and Neal the inside solution.

Their crises involved their total selves. Their dangers were perceived as anchored in their administrative situations, and their neurotic solutions were addressed to these severe stresses and strains. It is important to note that both practiced overcommitment. Neal elevated corporate authority to arbitrarily set corporate goals to the level of ultimate values. In the initial stage of his career crisis, he did not seek authority, and he set goals as a consequence of his achievement drive. Later, he administered his computer program to serve his growing obsession with power. The typical successful executive seeks first the joys of achievement and second the satisfaction of power, money, and status. Neal has primarilized the secondary satisfactions and practices association with the other remaining life areas.

Norman was overcommitted to business authority and organization too, which became to him ultimate values. The effects of his anxiety became displaced upon institutions outside of business. He practiced association with his administrative role as evidenced in his absentee administrative style. Not satisfied with dispensing authority and directing the goals of a single corporation, he set about to authorize and establish goals for society and, eventually, all of mankind. For that matter, Neal in his own way attempted to reset the course for mankind. Neal appealed to social Darwinism, and Norman to social responsibility. One wanted to make the world into a jungle, the other wanted to make it into a hospital. Neal chose the inside track and Norman the outside.

Neither philosophy of administration was grounded in the conditions of feasibility. What bothered Norman so terribly was that the business corporation was still a profit oriented organization and, in spite of his railing against it, he could not and basically did not want to make it into a social organization. His huge corporation had enough stability and power to afford the utilization of a wide selection of corporate purposes and policies beyond the traditional economic goals. In this sense, his social responsibility theme was in part grounded in factual achievements of the corporation. However, the corporation essentially was used to feed Norman's neurotic needs for love and affection. It became his vehicle of transportation into the outside world.

Neal's corporation, likewise, could order goals and policies affecting the aim of corporate citizenship. However, his neurosis drove him into a pattern of compulsive power-seeking. Power became the vehicle for executing his inside solution. It is interesting that after he became president, Neal tampered very little with the overall corporate goals and strategies. He sought power and, to avoid guilt, he attempted to legitimatize his power by appeals to the conventional notions of business authority. His board meetings always resounded with airs of respect for the property rights of stockholders, who were the legitimate authority and for whom he made his arbitrary decisions. This appeal was made in transparent mockery because some twenty thousand well-dispersed, unorganized, passive stockholders could not effectively levy claims upon his corporate administration. He ruthlessly replaced directors and was

But the men in this book did not pass through this danger zone alone. Their experiences were recorded by the author. In most cases he was the only confidant. Wives, relatives, ministers, doctors, friends, and colleagues were not usually confided in, and when they were they usually proved inept to guide them. Most of them did not understand the world of the big business executive. Their sympathies did not crack the shell of privity that incorporates the kind of personal tragedy that these executives experienced. Ministers glibly offered their themes of social and spiritual salvation. Wives were loyal but reserved and often bewildered. Even the arts of the medical profession were found wanting. Concepts and remedies of the more general medical disorders and of the more specialized psychotic disturbances proved nonspecific or unwieldly. More often than not, psychiatric expertise proved too authoritative, as when a ten-pound mallet is used to shatter thin ice. Or it was strangely coercive, as when a known solution is forced upon a novel problem. Mark Whiting was told by medical authority that he was sexually frustrated. Will Fowler was advised that he was suffering from a persecution complex. A psychiatric authority informed Oliver Dansby that he was a manic-depressive and should be hospitalized. Where calipers were needed, grappling hooks were provided. Where career advice was needed, libido theory was offered.

Because of the loneliness of their embattled lives, these executives offered to share their experiences with the readers who may be as unaware as they were. Hopefully, their experiences will help inexperienced and unsuspecting readers detect when a career crisis is a remote possibility, when it is imminent, the moment of impact, and the passing of it.

A summarization of their case histories reveals four crucial factors in the anatomy of a career crisis. These are the attacker, danger zone, target, and victim. The danger zone has two regions. The secondary region is where the executive has become a target of corporate wrath and abandonment. The primary region is the maximum impact area. Here the target has been successfully attacked and is now the victim. To feel like a victim he must feel victimized. Let us summarize the findings of this book by means of this typography of the mind of a typical crisis-stricken executive.

The danger zone is no particular position in the corporation.

It cannot be identified by the trappings of office, the strained faces of people, the risks of managerial assignments, or the warnings of authority figures. The danger zone is not identifiable by physical objects. It is foremost a psychological state of mind into which the executive enters with foreboding and apprehension.

The danger zone emerges in the executive's mind from a confrontation with the forces of his administrative world. This confrontation is not usually sought by the would-be target. Superiors and colleagues demand an investigation when events happen that are unexpected and unwanted. This is one of the oldest habits of organized society. Men demand explanation when things go awry and satisfy this urge by blaming somebody. Their target may be innocent or guilty. When a specific executive is singled out to bear the brunt of corporate wrath, the executive is set up to become a target.

All corporations have forces that wait to be activated against a target. It is much as though these forces are waiting for an emergency to strike, at which time they become natural to the environment. Men say and do things then that they would not without a target. Once given a target of administrative failure, the executive becomes a target of pent up energy, insecurity feelings, and guilt motives of many people incidental to his work. He becomes a target of unrelated human discontent. In some way, all targets are both innocent and guilty.

The executive may not know that he has been targeted. He does not know the attackers. The danger zone forms in his mind when information is communicated to him directly or indirectly by creditable and authoritative sources about his responsibility for the particular event. This mistake may be an act of omission or commission. He moves farther into the danger zone when he interprets this information as threatening to his present job and future career opportunities.

At this point he may sense who are his attackers. Typically, he will first underestimate the seriousness to self of the allegations. Also, he will discount the negative evaluations placed upon his act by his superiors. He is still not fully aware that he is a target. He may see that he is in trouble, but he has been in tight spots before. However, his instincts annoy him. He senses that there is more restlessness among his superiors and colleagues than is proper for a minor mistake. He senses a full-scale movement being organized against him. He concludes that this is no minor engagement.

When he realizes that he is in real trouble, he may set forth upon a search pattern. He may start his own investigation, utilizing friends, subordinates, and sometimes superiors removed from his area of responsibility. At this point, the men who helped with his attackers' investigation may be included in the target's investigation. The overlapping of these two search teams causes him to acquire confusing information. This information may temporarily mislead him to believe that his suspicions are ill-founded.

However, when he pauses to reflect upon the state of affairs he may decide that he is in real trouble. At this point he usually devises strategy to defend himself and to overcome his acts of omission or commission. Now the target is no longer stationary. He is exchanging and repelling verbal and written missiles. His combative posture causes the combat zone to widen and attract more attackers.

Meanwhile, the executive's solution to rectify his alleged mistake is met with belligerency. It turns out to be unproductive. This solution is of the kind that actually adds to his pattern of errors. Mark Whiting attempted to propose a drastic change in the corporation's direction and character. Will Fowler attempted to ignore the spirited stockholder group that moved against him. Perhaps if they had done nothing, their persons would have been less subject to heated attack. However, once members of a highly organized system set out to find a sacrificial lamb, they are not easily turned back.

The strategy of the target seems simple and benign enough. He decides to cover up his mistakes by a positive, constructive program of change or improvement. Such a strategy is aimed at authority figures who were attentive to the target's ambition and proposals in the past. Now many of them have joined the list of attackers and misunderstand the target's intentions. The target soon deserves his mistake.

The unproductive solution confirms the growing awareness of the superiors of the target that he is incompetent or untrustworthy, or both, and that they were right to ascribe responsibility to him for the original mistake. He is now in a state of emerging panic. His condition is observed by other members of the corporation and encourages them to offer evidence from his past or contrived evidence to assure that he appears incompetent or untrustworthy, or both. Some of these people will be past and present subordinates, superiors, and peers. A consensus of opinion sets in that the executive is working above his level of administrative capacity. Regardless of why he is attacked, the official reason is always this one. Attackers objectify the target's mistakes and their own intentions and motives. With the company manual in one hand and the sword of collective good in the other, attackers sacrifice their victims at the altar of administrative efficiency.

The point approaching the maximum impact area is reached when someone with the necessary power and authority decides that the executive is unworthy of further trust, support, and confidence and must be removed from the corporation or from the line of command. This individual is usually a rung or two higher than the superior who led the attack initially. A top level executive is usually demoted to a position not crucial to anyone in the corporation. He is placed on a corporate shelf. Here he has time to feel the full impact of his career difficulty. He remains in the maximum impact zone as long as he continues to think of himself as a victim.

However, for him to feel that he is a victim, a number of factors must converge simultaneously upon the target. The target must be aware of these forces. Foremost among these forces is the willingness on the part of sponsors and supporters of the target to withdraw their endorsement of him. Few executives move into the maximum impact area who maintain support from men in high positions. The second factor is the failure of his friends and peers to give him support. When superiors, peers, and friends fail to offer substantive support, he feels that he has had it. He is now a victim by his own admission.

All of this movement toward the maximum impact area nears culmination when the target comes to understand that he is not only being punished, but also abandoned. The point of abandonment by his supporters is also the point when he feels intensely the anxiety of inadequacy and uncertainty. The attack led by known and unknown men has found the target. They have achieved their objective. At this point the victim is left alone to discover for himself the total impact upon his career and life style. Success of the attack is represented by the emasculation of a once authoritative and powerful posture of the executive. He is now an administrative zero. (Review the case of Mark Whiting for insight into this life of a non-person.) To be sure, others may offer him the courtesies becoming of gentlemen. But he has no voice in the councils of administration.

It is interesting to note that vast resources are offered to individuals who work to succeed and keep a winning score. But few resources are offered to the failure. Although Mark Whiting became a minor recipient of corporate charity, little time and energy were expended to help him start his career all over again. No system was swung into action to help him find a meaningful job in his corporation or society. He was given a job that held out little hope and dignity for him. In contrast, great pains were taken to prepare and move the new president and his men into the right jobs. Rituals of celebration were performed for those who received the top promotions. Whiting was on his own. He had to find the means to recoup his losses, repair his wounded ego, and revive his drive to accomplish important tasks. The failures in this book were treated as blights that scarred the corporate landscape.

As a victim, the executive's career crisis has just begun. He has to develop a strategy to revive his career and regain his lost dignity. What he will do is not too predictable. But whatever he does, he will do it largely on his own. Hence, there is no way to identify a common pattern of career redemption. This is a basic finding that has been revealed in counseling. The forces that lie in a danger zone are not usually the forces that may be tapped to ameliorate the effects of career disaster. The corporation is a one-way street. If you succeed, you are served by a host of personnel who curry your favor. The whole human pyramid comes into action for the service of men at the top. The men who become victims are abandoned much as though their disease is communicable. The life of an administrative cipher is perpetual ignominy played in the key of corporate justice.

Men often mention the loneliness that visits executives at the top. However, the loneliness of the abandoned executive is without equal. It is his estranged and isolated position that causes the victim to clutch at any straw for relief from victimization. He may adopt the outside solution. We have seen that a career crisis often generalizes to the whole life style. Resources in the home, family, community, church, and social organizations may be utilized by the executive to avoid the ignominy of a cipher. The infinite kind and variety of these resources make impossible the standardizing of an exit pattern from the danger zone. When corporations will spend as much of their resources on the failures as they do on the successes, then perhaps victims will not have to withdraw psychologically and physically from their corporations in order to ward off the effects of their disasters.

Some executives stay in the danger zone for several years and others for the remainder of their careers. That is to say, they feel the impact of their career crisis over varying periods of time. Likewise, some executives become victims almost overnight and others become victims over a protracted period of time. The speed with which an executive penetrates the danger zone and acquires the mentality of a victim varies with the extent to which he is vulnerable. Some executives are more failure-prone than others. That is to say, they are more prone to make errors, to become targeted, and to become full-fledged victims. Each executive has a style of success. He has a habit of doing things right. If he did not have a success style, he could not have moved into an executive position. But little is ever said about the executive's style of error. By this is meant that he has a habit of repeating certain mistakes and of knowing occasionally when he is repeating them. Likewise, each executive has a style of risk. He habitually leaves certain things to intuition, imprecision, or sheer carelessness. Lastly, each executive has a style of chance. He has been unlucky to be at the wrong spot at the wrong time in his career. However, some seem to have more than the usual share of misfortune. It is almost as if they want to fail or be hurt in some way. The most thoughtful, deliberate, and organized executive has styles of error, risk, and chance. Anyone of these styles may cause him to become a target.

But not all targets become victims. Here a special style enters the picture. It is the style of panic. This quality most commonly identifies a victim. Few targets would become victims if they did not panic. To avoid victimization, the target must maintain the utmost equanimity in the face of imminent disaster. An air of detachment must pervade his mind in order to give maximum expression to reason. In addition, a cool head wards off the attackers. A target who maintains his self-control and confidence cannot be easily attacked. If he bears up well, attackers will tend to minimize and discount his previous mistakes. Because he shows strength that sustains their heaviest volleys, they begin to disengage from their aggressive pattern. It is only a target who feels and acts like a victim that attracts a disproportionate share of corporate wrath. Men who believe the target to be weak may attempt to prove it if given ever so slight an opportunity. In short, if a target believes that he is a victim, he will act and be treated like a victim.

Mark Whiting's Style of Panic

Panic is that state of mind that emerges when an individual begins to lose his self-confidence. There may be many reasons for an executive to become a target, and some of them are external to the executive. But a target becomes a victim largely because of defects and weaknesses that inhere in him. And his style of panic conforms to one of these inherent characteristics. Each victim displays a unique style. He may become hyperactive and violent, or emotional and depressed. He may dissolve before his superiors or he may issue threats and invectives. Many display a weird mixture of reason and emotion that appears perplexing and irrational to the bystander. Mark Whiting developed a violent reaction pattern, spliced occasionally by periods of servility. He first blamed others and in his later stages he blamed himself. For that matter, all victims eventually come to blame themselves. When they do, they self-validate their failures.

Panic causes gross mistakes to be made that in turn erode self-confidence. The victim becomes a failure in his own eyes. Let us listen to Mark Whiting's report on his style of panic.

I guess I wanted the presidency more than anything in my whole life. I was so near to it and yet I could feel it slipping away from me even before the new president was appointed. I guess I got desperate. I decided that no one was going to cheat me out of my life's work. I knew

The Failure-Prone Executive

better than to go around the retiring president and submit to the board my scheme of new goals for the corporation. But I lost control and in a moment of anger I fired off the proposal. I realize now that the board members who used my proposal were using me. I was hungry for support and mistook their eagerness to have me submit a proposal. Actually, they wanted someone to be their patsy and thought I would do. This blast at the president, and that was what my proposal was actually, led to other mistakes. I found myself getting in deeper and deeper. I would leave home in the morning resolved to keep cool, and by noon I was beside myself. Looking back on it all, I can see that I could have saved myself a lot of trouble at many points along the way. For example, I should have not accepted the invitation of Mr. Gray, the new president, to go to lunch with him every Tuesday and Thursday noon. But I was hungry for support; any kind would do. At first I thought I would use him. Then I became trapped by his sympathy and affection. It's funny, I would always start the lunch hour off in a big huff. Eventually I would become passive and then extremely courteous, bordering on affection for him. I repeated this pattern endlessly. With a minimum of investment on his part, Mr. Gray kept me at a distance from the corporation and himself. What a small cost to pay for my removal from his hair. Anyway, he completely emasculated me. He stripped me naked piece by piece. He took my pride; yes, my pride. What else would have allowed me to lean upon his every word and deed during our bi-weekly noon-hour ritual.

As the reader listens to this account, he may grasp the ignominy of Mark Whiting's defeat. He is blaming Mr. Gray for taking away his self-confidence and esteem. Listen to Whiting's remarks that were offered some time later.

Actually, I shot myself down. True, I made mistakes and should have been punished. But I alone destroyed my self-confidence. During our noon luncheons I let myself feed off of him in more ways than one. I just let myself go to pot. I didn't care anymore what people thought of me—the worse the better. Where it all started, I don't know. I believe it started when I decided that life meant one and only one thing to me—the presidency. I put all my eggs in one basket. I used to believe that my father was at fault, then my superiors, then the former president, then Mr. Gray. I guess I'm really the culprit.

At this point Whiting's victimization is complete. He feels that he became a victim by means of his own hands. Notice the style of panic. He alternated between episodes of blaming others and then blaming himself. Finally, he settled upon self-blame. If he had not proved his incompetency and untrustworthiness, he definitely did when he reported to others that he alone was to blame. He remarks:

> I decided that I should let Mr. Gray know. One day I told him at lunch that I was completely off base. I said that I must have been crazy to have done the things that I did. Anyway, I said that I had not been feeling my usual self for some time, and that I probably would have been tripped-up by the job of the presidency. I got such a positive reaction from Mr. Gray that I decided to tell others about my responsibility. I told one executive that no one was to blame but myself. At the time I must have really splattered myself, because I poured it on very heavy. But it was true. Of course, I realize that few men appreciate these kinds of admissions. I should not have spoken my thoughts. They knew that I was to blame anyhow. Saying it only made them aware of how little self-pride I had left.

Mark Whiting's panic lasted for several months. Actually, he had peak periods with intervals of relative rationality. As his extended periods of panic gradually subsided, his feelings of being under indictment and attack lessened. Eventually he did not feel that he was under any form of scrutiny or examination. He didn't feel that all eyes were upon him. He discovered that his colleagues and superiors had long forgotten his past difficulties. In fact, many of them had accepted him as a legitimate officer of the corporation soon after he had been appointed secretary of the board. He reasoned that if they had forgotten about his past, why could he not do the same. At this point, Mark Whiting ceased to be a victim. He was no longer in the hot seat.

But the danger zone through which he passed has not evaporated. Such a humiliating experience has left an indelible mark on his mind. Any situation that reminds him of the events that occurred before and during his career crisis causes him to feel slightly anxious. His fear that he will panic ever so slightly forces him to take certain necessary precautions. He reports, "I just look them (people who remind him of attackers) in the eye, straighten my back, take a deep breath, and attempt to take charge of the situation. I don't have any trouble if I do that." There will always be a danger zone in Mark Whiting's psychological makeup. A career crisis has this effect.

The cases in this book illustrate that each executive has a

tolerance for maintaining a sense of control under conditions of extreme threat or disaster. As a group they varied somewhat in their panic thresholds. A few were high, but more were low. The reasons why tolerances vary is still largely unknown. But the men in this book show several dispositions or tendencies that made for a high vulnerability to failure in the zone of maximum impact. In this central zone their styles of panic emerged. Let us see what caused them to panic and break lose from their emotional footings.

The Victim's Fear of Failure

The first vulnerability stems from the executive's inability to accept a career failure. He practices self-deceit in a curious fashion. The upward-striving manager is largely unaware that each promotion brings him closer to a life potentially filled with neurotic terror. He works hard to assume high positions in order to man-handle his corporation. He does not fully realize that this struggle to become the top man exposes his basic weaknesses. It is not that he is completely unaware of the terrors of a career crisis and the distortions it may bring to his style of life. His senses of threat and personal disaster are sufficiently keen. In fact, they are keen enough to prevent unreserved enjoyment of his achieved level of success. But his active fear of defeat prevents him from assessing the potential dangers ahead. This makes the upwardly mobile executive both anxious and ignorant about the potential dangers to his career and style of life.

In his mind the vulnerable executive does not associate success with failure. Many executives do, as was pointed out in previous chapters. But the vulnerable executive does not really accept as valid the possibility that the experience of failure is directly proportionate to the degree of success. Of course, he may speak about this possibility in public, but the probability that the higher one goes the harder one may fall is not seriously believed. He would rather believe that success progressively moves him away from the edge of failure. This logic drives him to achieve the pinnacle of corporate success. The presidential suite represents the farthest distance from failure. Success is where the president sits. Men with a black-white category of success must judge themselves to be failures when they do not achieve their aims in life.

Executives who believe that success belongs only to men at the top, are strongly disposed to regard the occupants of presidential suites as larger than life. They are viewed as perfected and completed. Their shortcomings are inverted to appear as strengths. This mechanism of inversion suggests a strong fear of accepting their worst suspicions of men and life at the top. This hero worship obstructs their powers of observation that would show that top men are oftentimes a prey to their own basic weaknesses. Actually, the top of the corporate ladder is for some the shortest distance to failure. The vulnerable executive senses this fact but is not capable of accepting or expressing it. He keeps a glamorized version of men and life at the top.

We have seen that the presidential suite may be occupied by an executive who is just one failure away from a total breakdown. The practice of counseling executives suggests that the top position exposes men to their weaknesses more than to their strengths. The striving for success is a neurosis more often than the success-driven executive is willing to admit.

We have seen that the topmost job can bring on neurotic tendencies that warp the executive's judgment and distort his company. Positions eagerly sought after at any level may have the same effect. However, positions below the president are greater in number and carry with them fewer risks and lesser responsibilities. The neurotic potential in the presidency is compounded by its single occupancy, its vast authority and power, its grave risks and responsibilities, and its widespread attractiveness to managers and executives many of whom are both anxious and ignorant about these features.

Of course, men are attracted to the presidency for various reasons. Foremost among these motives is the desire to achieve results for and through others. Others are attracted to the office of president because of its presumed magic ability to dispel fears of failure and personal catastrophe. These men are inwardly weak and seek the office of the president to make them feel strong. The presidency is their crutch without which they have no effective means of support.

The neurotic potential in the office of the presidency is the product of the stresses of the office and the weaknesses of the men who may occupy it. The office of the president may cause the healthy to apply their mature skills, and it may encourage the unhealthy to utilize their neurotic devices. Some executives become organizationally successful in spite of their neuroses and others because of them. The latter executive was described in the previous chapter as "neurocratic."

The Victim's Illusion of Immunity

The second vulnerability follows closely from the first. Most executives who have not experienced a career crisis hold an attitude of immunity. They don't feel that a career crisis and the experiences of executives described in this book could ever happen to them. On the other hand, executives who have been through a career crisis cannot understand why others about them have not been exposed to such humiliating and terrifying experiences. The experienced cannot understand why they have been selected from among others who are more deserving. The inexperienced cannot understand why others take career blows as hard as they do.

Counseling evidence suggests that some executives hold a high sense of immunity that borders on an illusion. Will Fowler is a case in point. He knew of men who were demoted or fired and assumed that they returned to normal living after a brief period of shock. He never believed that they behaved irrationally over prolonged periods of time. As he looks back on himself, he realizes that he was terribly naive. He held a naive faith in his own powers to take himself in hand and master the threat in good time.

Executives who have an unqualified belief in immunity from the ravages of a career crisis increase the risk of being overwhelmed. When their feelings of security and mastery become shattered, they have nothing to fall back upon. On the other hand, executives who have a qualified sense of immunity are apt to admit that a career crisis could ruin their whole life. They learn to live with this possibility and retain the belief that they will somehow survive. They are more apt to emerge from the danger zone with less emotional disturbance and more apt to avoid becoming a victim. Anticipation is a kind of rehearsal in imagination and can have an inoculating effect.

An illusion of immunity has one other disadvantage. The executive shows a sluggish or sloppy response to the preliminary warnings that typically precede a career crisis. Will Fowler was very slow to size up the implications of not immediately replacing the deceased president. He also showed a tardy response to the animosity and resistance of the new stockholder group that eventually kicked him out of the corporation. Will Fowler became victimized by his illusion of immunity.

In short, the executive's illusion of immunity hastens his career crisis and diminishes his powers of mastering it. The vulnerable executive feels the least vulnerable. It is also clear that executives who hold a total belief in immunity acquire a more intense fear of repetition of a career crisis after they have once experienced it. It follows that an experienced executive feels the most vulnerable.

The Victim's Illusion of Mastery

The third characteristic of a vulnerable executive is his illusion of mastery. He feels that he can handle any success or failure in his life, including catastrophes at work, home, and in the community. Executives who feel total mastery usually have had few, if any, real failures in their careers. Some have climbed the corporate ladder rapidly and have not stayed long enough in any position to reveal their latent weaknesses and to have their real achievements evaluated.

Other executives acquire a sense of omnipotence from actually achieving superhuman tasks. They know that they are thoroughly competent because they have had their skills tested. What they fail to realize is that while their administrative skills have been subjected to rigorous testing, their psychological skills to cope with subjective stress may have escaped comparable testing. A career crisis is a subjective state of mind and, hence, is foremost a test of internal control and stability. Consequently, executives may not have had their characters tested if they have merely overcome managerial blocks no matter how rigorous they might have been.

It is only when executives have undergone targeting and victimization that their styles of panic can be assessed fully. The fact that they did surmount managerial blocks successfully may be taken as support for the idea that they have not learned to cope with personal catastrophe. Only the victims of career crisis are aware with some degree of certainty of what skills they have to cope with their personal catastrophes. They are aware of their panic thresholds.

The illusion of omnipotence is acquired in part from being near-misses of a career crisis. Near-misses are men who stand near or next to targets and victims. They observe how victims have enlarged and prolonged their career difficulties. They have objectivity unbecoming of a real victim. The near-misses believe that they can assess what the crisis-stricken executive did wrong and that they can learn from their observations. With each near-miss they grow more confident that if attacked they can successfully defend themselves. Their illusion of omnipotence grows with their opportunity and capacity to observe the behavior of victims. Then, too, the more they are missed, the more they believe they will be missed. Some get downright cocky.

The illusion of immunity and omnipotence work hand in glove. The former says, "I cannot be a target of corporate hostility, punishment, and abandonment." The latter says, "If perchance I become a target, I can masterfully rearrange my affairs or the situation, or both, to restore my career opportunity. Hence, I certainly will avoid becoming a victim."

The less vulnerable executive observes carefully the behavior of victims about him. He acquires a belief that he will do his best and that if the worst comes to him, he will not lose his capacity to accept reality. He is prepared to muster certain strategies and skills to restore his career drive, even though the situation appears to exceed his capacity. Such a view greatly prohibits the feeling of total loss of mastery that inheres potentially in every career crisis. When the vulnerable executive's sense of omnipotence becomes shattered, he reverts to a feeling of total inadequacy and despairs that there is little, if anything, he can do. At this point he becomes a prey to his self-suspicions and doubts and endangers his chances of surviving. His style of panic takes over to victimize him.

The Victim's Illusion of Support

The fourth characteristic of a vulnerable executive is his illusion of support. He believes that if he does get into career difficulty, there will be someone around who will help him or who will ameliorate the disturbances to his career and life. Mark Whiting had his friends, some of whom were members of the outside board, others were his subordinates, and a few were his peers. He thought that all of them would stand by him if things went bad for him. However, none of this support emerged when he needed it most. There were periods when lack of support caused him more internal anguish than his basic career difficulty.

The experienced executive knows that members of his corporation will not interject themselves into an affair of corporate punishment and abandonment. The few who will are usually powerless and incapable of performing meaningful acts of interposition. A career crisis is intensified when a high sense of support is shattered by the self-centered motives of so-called friends.

It seems that when one executive becomes a target of punishment and abandonment, others turn their aroused energies toward themselves just as the victim does. A career crisis becomes in part a crisis for every executive exposed to the victim. Each member invests more energy in his work for a period of time after the target has been attacked. By doing this he tends to propitiate the powers to be and maintain his sense of mastery over his own career. By not giving support to the victim, he does not become a secondary or innocent target. Hence, he keeps his high sense of immunity. He also foregoes testing his powers to endure a career crisis because he stands apart from the turbulence surrounding a colleague's personal catastrophe. Ignorance of his own style of panic is preserved.

The illusion of support may be kept alive long after support for the victim fails to emerge. Executives on the outside of the disaster scene are usually impelled to visit the victim. They are mostly curious to find out what has happened. If the victim is a competitor or hostile colleague, curiosity may be joined by sadistic delight in knowing how the victim was targeted and how badly he is taking the attack. In some cases, associates of the victim may manifest consideration for him and share verbally in his fears and anxieties. These remarks are gratuities but may be interpreted by the victim to mean support. Actually, they are often altruistic claims to brotherhood and do not carry the weight of practical steps and do little to relieve the victim of his panic and crisis.

The Victim's Illusion of Explanation

The fifth characteristic of a vulnerable executive resides in the tendency to avoid and master catastrophe by attributing to it causes that appeal to his powers of manipulation and control. The catastrophe of death is a good example. When someone dies, it is because he did something or something was done to him. He may have been obese, sinful, or careless with his body. He may have failed to get prompt medical help, disobeyed doctor's orders, prolonged his illness by self-pity. He may have been driving his car carelessly, going too fast, or driving an unsafe vehicle. When he attributes death to a cause that is within the province of human control, death loses its reality and sting for him.

Likewise, the vulnerable executive attributes to another's career crisis specific causes of such a nature that reduce his own chances of having one. The victim disobeyed orders, did not get the facts, was too careless with his subordinates, etc. Each of the factors could have prevented a career crisis because they seem amenable to human intelligence and manipulation.

In most cases, the causes are seen to emanate from the misconduct of the victim. Seldom is the corporation held to be errant. It has been the observation of the author that the corporation can do no wrong. It is seldom blamed for the personal tragedy of an executive. The blame lies with the target. To avoid becoming a target, the executive needs only to account for these causes of a career crisis. The author has yet to meet an executive who cannot afix to a colleague's personal tragedy a set of known causes. It is only the target who is usually less certain about what has happened to him.

The consequences to an executive who has the illusion of explanation is that he usually abides by his beliefs. If he encounters a career crisis which cannot be explained by his beliefs of causation, his senses of security and mastery are shattered. He may report that there was absolutely no reason for him to become a target of corporate wrath. He is next apt to complain that he did not deserve to be a victim and that he was unjustly singled out for demonstration purposes. It is true that when things go wrong, business executives feel compelled to find a target for relieving themselves of responsibility. Someone always becomes a target and, occasionally, the target becomes an innocent victim. But whether he is innocent or not, the target is still a target and must face such a reality. Failure to face reality may cause behavior to occur that justifies in its own right corporate hostility and punishment. The illusion of explanation enhances the probability that an executive will become a major cause of his own career crisis. The executive may become victimized by his own pat explanations.

The Victim's Unbalanced Triangle

The sixth characteristic of a vulnerable executive is based upon a basic imbalance in his administrative style. Many executives are only dimly aware that they are authority-centered or organization-centered or self-centered. It is characteristic of executives to find compensating skills for the weaknesses of an unbalanced corporate triangle. By finding substitutes the unbalanced nature of their administrative style is preserved. Extending the life of an unbalanced style may bring career disaster in the future. All that is needed is a situation which cannot be successfully approached by the compensating skills. This situation will prove to be immune to these, and it will also tap the inherent weaknesses found in the authority- organization-, or self-centered patterns. An unbalanced executive in the throes of a frustrating administrative solution is a prey to his basic weaknesses. The inevitable result is an attentuation of his unbalanced AOS frame to extreme and oftentimes ridiculous proportions which become visible to all other members of the authority set who have the power to release corporate hostility and to execute acts of collective abandonment. Mark Whiting and Will Fowler stretched their AOS frames to such ridiculous proportions that their opponents gathered support for their abandonment from the most neutral quarters of the corporation's board and stockholder group.

The less vulnerable executive is apt to have a realistic awareness of his basic administrative deficiencies. For the sake of success he is apt to attack these weaknesses rather than spin off elaborate compensations. The reader will recall that this is what Will Fowler eventually came to do. He dropped his rationalizations for his unbalanced administrative style, rejected his long established compensations, and addressed himself to his authority-centered corporate triangle.

The less vulnerable executive is not strongly suspicious of authority or incapable of believing in the reality of organizational life. Nor is he strongly deferential toward superiors and rigidly loyal to the existing goals and ends of the corporation. He respects the reigns of authority and the men who legitimately hold them in their hands. This deference allows the upwardly mobile manager to work hard for superiors and to learn from them. At the same time, he holds moderate distrust of superiors so as to feel the necessity to exert independent, innovative effort in his own behalf. He works hard to innovate and actively seeks and keeps the support of his superiors. The less vulnerable executive does both well.

The less vulnerable executive believes in corporate effort. He comes prepared to believe in teamwork and the necessity of playing circumscribed roles in organizational activity. He believes in the need to sacrifice for total effort, in the continuity of the firm, in the systematic posting and executing of reasonable rules and regulations. The less vulnerable executive does not defer to the imperatives of organized effort to the extent that he cannot attack the posted goals, objectives, and policies, and seek to have them changed. His moderate distrust of the *status quo* allows for change and innovation.

We have observed that the less vulnerable executive ascribes qualities to himself that come from real achievement. His self-image is grounded in reality. The vulnerable executive has notions of self that emanate from fantasy and wish-fulfillment. His idealized self prevents realistic assessment of his strengths and weaknesses. When faced with a difficult situation, his strengths fail to show and his weaknesses appear without compensation. The less vulnerable executive has productive notions of self. Their utility is found in his capacity to achieve in reality the potentialities that have accrued from his many past performances.

In effect, the unbalanced executive allows his achievement drive to be too much or too little directed by any one component of the corporate triangle. Career difficulty may develop eventually. The probability of career crisis is high, but not sufficient to guarantee it. The unbalancing of the corporate triangle is a necessary but not sufficient cause of career crisis. The necessary causes inhere in the situation. Perhaps if another person had been president, if another person besides Mr. Gray had succeeded to the presidency, Mark Whiting would be more alive career-wise than he is today. A career crisis is a marriage between the man and his environment. Others may single him out to be a target, but the executive contributes a great deal to making himself into a victim.

The cases of Neal and Norman illustrate how a career crisis may not restore the balanced posture of the executive. Under the right circumstances, an unbalanced executive may actually be promoted to the top position. Also, Neal and Norman had sufficient internal controls to disguise their distorted orientations. Mark Whiting apparently did not. His distrust of authority became too apparent, whereas Neal and Norman were able to hide their neurotic tendencies by latching onto favorable situational circumstances. Their neuroses actually exploited an emerging situation. More typically, however, an unbalanced orientation will prevent mobility to the top. The unbalancing of the corporate triangle and the presence of individuals who may react negatively to the distortions spell career difficulty.

Conclusion: The Tyranny of the Success Habit

The foremost conclusion of this study is that life in the big business corporation is an emotional experience that cannot be approximated by life in any other institution in our society. Most men who arrive at the top have at one time been pulled away or nearly pulled away from their emotional anchorages. However, the exact number who have failed to master their career crisis is not known. In the opinion of the author, the number is very large. What attracts men to the corporation is the tremendous opportunity to achieve. Foremost among these achievement opportunities is upward mobility. The large corporation appears as a formidable pyramid, complete with the necessary ladders for efficient scaling. But it is more treacherous than it looks. Nevertheless, the corporate pyramid attracts large numbers of both ignorant and anxious men. Many are unbalanced. These men are vulnerable. Their inability to accept their fears of failure, their illusions of immunity, omnipotence, support, and explanation, and their distorted notions of authority, organization, and self are symptoms of their neurotic attachment to the success habit.

This neurotic success drive affirms the notion that to succeed one must bear an economic function. This means that one should be enterprising and should get ahead of one's fellows. One is what one does, and the tangible evidence of what one does is what one has. Work and the tangible rewards of achievement have become so central to our society that those who are not working or who have difficulty in their work are considered disturbed. Even psychiatrists have acquired the success mentality. They assume, as a rule, that the person who does not work is ill, and that the ability to work is once more evidence of the recovery of mental health.

In our society, work is considered to be therapeutic, and those who suffer incipient neuroses may actually allay or avert them by the pursuit of economic gain. The neurocrat is a manifestation of this phenomenon. In contrast, those who strive for economic security are often viewed as developing a neurotic defense mechanism as a symptom of a deeper emotional insecurity. Denial of the immediate pleasure drives in favor of long-term occupational goals is assumed to be both an ultimate social value and an indicator of mental maturity. Upward mobility and achievement are assumed to be a natural desire of man.

Thus, everyone must work usefully in order to maintain his mental health. When a man moves upward, he may incur a neurosis, but if he moves downward, he may pay the heavier penalty of psychosis. For this reason, the men who have achieved greatly, such as big business executives, are viewed by many today as superior psychological specimens. This book attempts to refute the widespread belief that men at the top of big business corporations are at the top of the ladder of psychological development. Many are neurotic, immature, unstable, terror-stricken, and irresponsible.

The vulnerable executive dreams in high gear. He pits his whole self against the corporate framework. He believes that success will come through devotion to hard work. He expects to realize in hard work mobility to the top and symbols of power, status, and privilege. His formula for success is simple. For every contribution to the firm, he will get a reward in kind. Success is a function of the individual's capacity to work. Failure is seldom a function of society and the corporate environment. If he succeeds, he takes the credit; if he fails, it is because he did not play the game well. This logic, found in the illusion of explanation, marks the failure-prone executive.

When the vulnerable executive becomes trapped by a seemingly unsoluble career crisis, he usually continues to rely too heavily upon work. We have seen how this pattern of work addiction releases sterile energy. He may repeat the unproductive solution endlessly or he may seek another version of work magic. This may be politics, community, statesmanship, or feverish religiosity. The cases in this book illustrate how the victims of a career crisis attempt to reorder their lives along different values. These new modes are eagerly sought, not for their intrinsic value, but for their instrumental value. They are cultivated for the purpose of relieving the career crisis. At the same time, these new ways of behaving in the corporation, home, and community keep alive the success drive. In religious, social, familial, or community endeavors the vulnerable executive attempts to find the solution to his career crisis. The solution is less outside of himself than inside.

Success is more than merely trying. Executives who move into the presidential suites of big business corporations leave perched on the lower rungs of the corporate ladder many managers and executives who try hard, work hard, compete hard. When an executive's whole personality is nucleated around the success habit, he sets himself upon a collision course with others who are equally ambitious. Hopefully, this collision course will lead to a confrontation with his self. During such a confrontation, the executive may discover how shallow his life has been. He may discover no real, acceptable self upon which to reconstruct his life. This self-discovery is to be desired because then he can proceed to gather a new set of values and beliefs and execute a search for a more meaningful identity. Only a few executives achieve meaningful self-confrontations. Those that do execute remarkable changes in their careers and life styles. They achieve new identities much as though they were reborn. An honest self-confrontation carries this experience of rebirth. It is the universal hallmark of the therapeutic acts.

Unfortunately, the neurotic success drive prevented many men in this book from confronting their naked selves. Without this level of insight into their private world of values and needs, reconstruction of a new style of living produces a facade. Many men in this book live today with new faces. Mark Whiting has taken on new assignments in his career and community. Yet, he cannot help but regret his many failures. He slips occasionally into states of depression at which time he severely attacks himself for having acted so stupidly. In other words, he did not and could not disturb his neurotic drive to succeed. He could not openly attack and relegate it to a lower position in his scheme of values. Will Fowler has a new face, too. He appears to be more human and permissive in his corporate world. He, too, failed to touch the central core of his personality. His success drive has not been diluted. He would rather be dead than remain in a position below the presidency of his corporation. Both Mark Whiting and Will Fowler have acquired new tactics with which to achieve the same strategic goals.

The point to be made is not that the success habit is bad. One may argue that it is both good and bad. Rather, the point is that many men who climb the corporate ladder are so neurotically anchored to the success habit that they cannot break their moorings to such a formidable practice. They cannot give priority to another value. We have seen that if any one of the executives in this study could have unchained themselves from their ideals of success, they could have adjusted themselves to a less prestigious life.

In place of destroying or diluting substantially the success habit, the goal to which it is attached is usually changed. For example, the executive may decide to engage in political, social, or religious work. We called this pattern the outside solution. Into these endeavors he will thrust his whole self, much as he did in his corporate career. He must do his best, work hard, improve his skills, and achieve more and different things than his predecessors. It is the same thing all over again in a different role. The success habit is still there, grinding out human energy and emotion.

Oliver Dansby is a case in point. If he had his way, few professors would be in their ivory towers. They would be active in their communities, acquiring and utilizing their knowledge by providing direct benefits to man and society. Oliver Dansby had one of the most frank confrontations with self of any man in this book. Nevertheless, he must become the best and most successful of the new activist type of professor that is emerging in the academic world.

One wonders seriously if there is anyone who approaches any occupational role obliquely, passively, and reservedly; who seeks to become involved but not immersed in either the achievement opportunities or the rewards of money, position, and fame. Our society is littered with individuals who are driven by one or the other. Men work hard to achieve great challenges with little eye toward money, fame, and security. Others work carelessly and indifferently but expect to realize high wages and fringe benefits. Their commitment is to the by-products of achievement. Few are the men who approach both sides of success with detachment and passivity. All men are expected to be committed to the habit of success. Men must be driven by something or they are not men.

The large business corporation as much as any modern institution is a creature of its times. It is the recipient of the many useful products that the success habit provides. In turn, it helps to attract and breed people with the neurotic success habit. Many activities in the corporation help to attract and breed neurotic executives, among them being the fact of mobility itself. The last decade has brought unheralded economic growth and prosperity. Men have moved up faster and in greater numbers than during any previous decade. The success habit was firmly established in the American male personality before this decade of spectacular growth. But the tremendous opportunities for success that it has opened up and the fact of open and rapid upward mobility have induced a dangerous unbalancing of life values. The bitch-goddess of success sits firmly and securely in the driver's seat. With a bull whip in one hand and the reins held taut in the other, she unmercifully prods her worshippers to greater and greater acts of devotion. She has become splendidly wicked.

In the path left by this awesome economic spiral lie many victims mangled by the competitive struggle to go farther and faster than their parents and their peers. These victims are largely without empathetic support. The American male, particularly the big business executive, does not really understand the Mark Whitings and cannot extend to them the dignity that they anxiously seek. There are many Mark Whitings who remain ambulatory in their corporations and communities, held upright by hope and wish-fulfillment, or fantasy and repression. Some sit on nicely prepared corporate shelves solving problems that do not need to be solved. They become mentally sloven and corpulant as meaningless activity erodes their self-respect. So frequently does the author meet these victims that he often speculates about the question, What will happen to the brittle personalities of these victims if an economic recession sets in of the magnitude that requires a major cutback in managerial personnel at all levels? Suppose economic necessity required weeding them out by the thousands? What will happen to men who have barely survived the turbulent experience of a career crisis and are held together by the corporate securities and gratuities made possible by a prosperous economy?

And what will happen to men who become targets and victims for the first time? There is a new generation of managers moving into high places in the large business corporation. They are too young to know about the prewar years and the great depression. They are the progeny of prosperity. In them the success habit thrives unchecked by the anxieties and fears of economic deprivation. They are the most vulnerable of the vulnerables. It remains to be seen how these young, upwardly mobile managers experience their career crises and what will be the consequences to their corporations, to society, and to themselves. However, one thing seems certain. A large number of the failure-prone executives will undergo the terrors of a career crisis.

155.926
J442e

WITHDRAWN
from
Funderburg Library